STORIES FROM PURANAS

Part 3

KAUSHAL KISHORE

KAUSHAL KISHORE

ISBN-13: 9798313495576
ISBN-10: 1477123456

Cover design by: Art Painter
Library of Congress Control Number: 2018675309
Printed in the United States of America

I Dedicate this book to
My Grandmothers Smt Anoopa Devi and Smt Ramcharita Devi,
My mother Smt Shanti Devi,
My elder sister Smt Veena Sinha
My wife Smt Sushma Kishore,
And all womens supporting me

CONTENTS

PROLOGUE

श्री गणेशाय नमः

नार्यस्तु राष्ट्रस्य श्वः ।

The ladies are the creators of the tomorrow,
or the future of a nation.

Most Indians now know widely the impact of destruction of our great Universities and education centers combined with burning of books and butchering of great scholars during end of eleventh century by savage foreign attackers, on education and research.

India was thereafter under the control of one or other hostile colonizing forces on major part of our country. The impact on social front was not less severe.

We, people educated under the Macaulay system of education (continuing in independent India), never knew the true impact, and assumed that our social ills resulted from some inherent weaknesses, and not because of planned negative policies and cruelty unleased by these colonial forces.

None of the famous historians has written what Max Mueller had told in 1884, "I say once more that I do not wish to represent the people of India as two hundred and fifty-three millions of angels, but I do wish it to be understood and to be accepted as a fact, that the damaging charge of untruthfulness brought against that people is utterly unfounded with regard to ancient times. It is not only not true, but the very opposite of the truth. As to modern times, and I date them from about 1000 after Christ (AD), I can only say that, after reading the accounts of the terrors and horrors of Mohammedan rule, my wonder is that so much of native virtue and truthfulness should have survived. You might as well expect a mouse to speak the truth before a cat, as a Hindu before a Mohammedan judge."

The omission to highlight occurred because the normal tendency of our historians to hide such cruel acts of our erstwhile rulers.

Like any other colonial powers, these foreign rulers made all out efforts to negate our history, and to deride and degrade our cultural and religious heritage. While Sanskrit education became popular in European countries and in USA for extracting pearls of wisdom from our ancient books written in Sanskrit, it lost support in India, when Britishers adopted new education system of Macaulay in 1835.

As earlier education system was derecognized and stopped, the colonial government was very successful in ensuring that Sanskrit, and great Indian scriptures were not read and known by normal educated Indians.

Even the independent Indian government was happy to continue the colonial education system, and books written by them deriding our culture were not corrected, despite having powers to decide for welfare of country.

The result of forgetting our basic culture, and history has been very devastating. Majority of Hindus now feel proud in deriding and demeaning their own culture, without actually knowing it.

Educated persons ape the Western culture because of their wrong education. Media, including mass-media, having profiteering motives is also presenting our culture in distorted forms.

A large population is under the spiderweb of false ideas propagated by education system and media, and sinking into lower and lower depths of superstition, not knowing the true base, the eternal wisdom of Sanatan Dharma.

It is essential to ensure that our culture, history and eternal pearls of wisdom and ideas are accessible and popularized among students and for that matter, all Indians.

I am now ashamed to accept that I was also highly critical of my own religion during my education period, while admiring the so-called reforms by British Government, particularly to educate women and improve the plight of Hindu women and widows.

I also admired the continued crusade by intellectuals, who quoted several lines from Manu Smriti, Gita, and Ramcharitmanas, and opined that Hinduism is against the freedom and equality of its women folk, and women are prohibited to read Veda, Gayatri Mantra, and other scriptures.

However, whenever I looked away from my books, I found very contrary position. My grandmother was queen of my house, and there was huge respect for my mother, my aunts, my sisters, and all women in my neighborhood. Similar was the situation in the house of my maternal grandmother.

Women in my family, were not only reading, but actually taught me Gayatri mantra and Hanuman Chalisa, and I heard many stories of Puranas, Mahabharata and Ramayana, and even of Hitopadesa, Akbar- Birbal, and others.

So, there was a great chasm between my knowledge from books and my observed truth. However, I reconciled by assuming that it was the result of the reforms made by British Government, since no reforms have been attributed to the governments after independence.

Also, women in my family were educated while the normal women literacy rate in my state Bihar was less than fifteen percent in nineties. I had the opportunity to work for the poorest of women in Gaya district. I found that despite being illiterate, and no special facilities, those Musahar women forming Self Help Groups were no less intelligent and virtuous.

I have observed that all villagers are regularly worshipping a number of goddesses. There is a Chandi pith in the temple of the village, where we go for prayer. Earlier, the goddess was represented by only a Pindi of mud, but later we had a large idol also.

We are praying to Durga, Saraswati, and Laxmi, and also Sita, Radha, and Parvati. Whether such worship of women power started by our reformers?

Only after reading from sources other than the course books prescribed for study, I could obtain clarity about the position of women in Hinduism, and comparative very poor position in other religious groups, who do not have any respect for Goddess in their culture.

I am now sure, I was not alone, rather this type of contrary and negative thinking is prevalent among all sincere students in India reading the prescribed books for degree or for competing in civil service examinations of India.

Through the narrative and stories in first two parts of the series, we have already examined and proved false the stated role of Puranas in caste division, and discrimination in first part of the series. Further, we have also examined the shame attached to idol worship by propagandists.

I herewith present the third part exclusively centered on the stories of the great Indian Women, Rishikas, sages and Goddesses from our ancient scriptures. In this part of the series, we explore and examine the actual position of women in Indian society in ancient times vis-à-vis the wrong information circulated among intellectuals by intellectuals with vested interest.

So, this third part of the series of books on Puranas is dedicated to the great women of our ancient culture. The scope of the book has been widened from stories from Puranas to include the description and stories of women sages and Goddesses in Vedas and Upanishads also.

This is my small step to remember and learn from their lives and stories. Let us, as a society adopt our great culture giving respect, equality and divinity to women.

CHAPTER 1
INTRODUCTION

Story 1 Macaulay education system

No body can deny the fact that women in India, in rural as well as in urban areas, are often the victims of crimes. We are seeing so many examples of such atrocities regularly despite passing of stricter rules, and other efforts of Government. But what is the reason? Whether it is our Sanatan Dharma or basic culture of India, or something else?

There had been a widespread effort by our British masters through the Macaulay education system (copied and continued by independent India) to glorify our colonial masters through the books written by their historians.

The basic education of Sanskrit and ancient scriptures was stopped by British, when they introduced the new Macaulay Education system.

These books also prove that India was backward till some Indians received English education. And our scholars and government made no efforts to check and correct the text books and the education system, even after our independence.

Story 2 Role of Max Muller

It is now well-known that British had deputed Max Muller to translate Vedas which was in Sanskrit language into English. Along with this Max Muller also had the responsibility to indoctrinate the Indians into believing that what they are considering as the basis of their Religion is filled with filth.

This was planned to ensure that the Hindus would start

doubting their sacrosanct Vedic literatures, would start feeling more inferior and will then easily accept the doctrines of British Colonists.

He was also forced to prove the baseless Aryan Invasion theory to divide Indians.

Max Muller's vicious agenda is not hidden after coming to light the letters he wrote. To his wife, he wrote, "It (the Rig Veda) is the root of their religion and to show them what the root is, I feel sure, is the only way of uprooting all that has sprung from it during the last three thousand years."

He observed, "The translation of the *Veda* will hereafter tell to a great extent on the fate of India, and on the growth of millions of souls in that country. It is the root of their religion, and to show them what the root is, I feel sure, is the only way of uprooting all that has sprung from it during the last 3,000 years."

On August 25th 1866, Muller wrote to Chevalier Bunsen:

"India is much riper for Christianity than Rome or Greece was at the time of St. Paul. The rotten tree has for some time had artificial supports, because its fall would have been inconvenient for the government. But if the Englishman comes to see that the tree must fall, sooner or later, then the thing is done."

In 1868 he wrote to George Campbell, the newly appointed Secretary of State for India:

"India has been conquered once, but India must be conquered again, and that second conquest should be a conquest by education. Much has been done for education of late, but if the funds were tripled and quadrupled, that would hardly be enough (...) The missionaries have done far more than they themselves seem to be aware of, nay, much of the work which is theirs they would probably disclaim. The Christianity of our nineteenth century will hardly be the Christianity of India. But the ancient religion of India is doomed—and if Christianity does not step in, whose fault will it be?

He used his links with the Brahmo Samaj to encourage a

reformation from within on the lines pioneered by **Ram Mohan Roy**. Müller believed that the Brahmos would engender an Indian form of Christianity and that they were in practice "Christians, without being Roman Catholics, Anglicans or Lutherans".

It was another story that he succeeded only partially in his mission, of introducing discord among Indians, and conversion of Hindus. Unfortunately, the AIT (Aryan Invasion theory), the myth populated by him without any proof, is still having blind supporters.

To be true to his genius, it must be stated that it was his thinking, and faith that was hugely impacted by study of Vedas. He, after completing the project, became very much appreciative of Hindu culture, and Sanskrit.

Do you read in any book what he told in his series of lectures, "What can India teach us?" at University of Cambridge. He championed India during 1883, as follows,

"If I were to look over the whole world to find out the country most richly endowed with all the wealth, power, and beauty that nature can bestow—in some parts a very paradise on earth —I should point to India. If I were asked under what sky the human mind has most fully developed some of its choicest gifts, has most deeply pondered on the greatest problems of life, and has found solutions of some of them which well deserve the attention even of those who have studied Plato and Kant—I should point to India."

He told in 1884 about the true nature of Indians as truthfulness. His such praise of Hinduism and Sanskrit language was, undoubtedly, against the colonial interest. This was why he was vehemently opposed by Church.

Monsignor Alexander Munro, an officer of the Roman Catholic Church in Scotland (and Provost of the Catholic Cathedral of Glasgow from 1884 to 1892), declared that Müller's lectures "were nothing less than a crusade against Divine revelation, against Jesus Christ, and against Christianity".

The blasphemous lectures were, he continued, "the proclamation of atheism under the guise of pantheism" and "uprooted our idea of God, for it repudiated the idea of a personal God".

As a result, his last writings and lectures were almost banned by the British government, and our Indian historians, were happy with his earlier saying against our wisdom only.

During their reign in India, the Britishers continued their anti-Vedic teachings. Among the Indians they only allowed those scholars to be part of the academic institutions who agreed with their viewpoints.

As negative writings against our culture and scriptures were rewarded through various awards, postings and positions, it was adopted by most of the Indians educated under the system.

These academicians, picked and indoctrinated by the British Colonists, later continued dominating the educational institutions even after India achieved independence.

They continue to make all efforts to ensure that, "Truth must hide herself; common sense must disappear from the field so that such a theory may flourish!"

So, a few lines from Manu Smriti, Ramayana and Mahabharata were identified by them and forming a caucus, they presented these lines proving ills of our culture in very planned way.

These few lines and their interpretations are being regularly referred by this group of scholars to show that the ill-treatment of women and their bad condition was because of the basics of Hindu religion.

Particularly women of India have been shown as very backward and suffering a lot because of the wrong thoughts and system prevailing in Hinduism.

Story 3 What our Scriptures say about women

Let us now explore the sayings about the women in the ancient texts, particularly the Vedas, Upanishads, Puranas and Tantras. Why not to start with the much-maligned Manu Smriti? There is a shloka in the third chapter of Manu Smriti:

यत्र नार्यस्तु पूज्यन्ते रमन्ते तत्र देवताः ।

यत्रैतास्तु न पूज्यन्ते सर्वास्तत्राफलाः क्रियाः ॥

(Manu smriti – 3.56)

It simply means that, "Devatas (gods) reside where women are respected (worshipped). Where women are not respected, all actions and dharma come to naught (do not bear fruits)."

Can anyone show a similar line from the books of other religions?

The importance given to women and their significance in society, is clear through such shlokas in Hindu scriptures, shedding light on their wisdom, strength, and influence.

Some others are quoted below:

पूजनीया महाभागाः पुण्याश्च गृहदीप्तयः ।

स्त्रियः श्रियो गृह्स्योक्ताः तस्माद्रक्ष्या विशेषतः ॥

As the women are the forebearer of great opulence, and virtue and bring splendor as well as respect and wealth to the house, they are respectable and their safety must be ensured especially.

It was prescribed as a proper social behavior by the Manu-Samhita that "A woman should be given protection at every stage of life. She should be given protection by the father in her younger days, by the husband in her youth, and by the grownup sons in her old age."

However, we are now fully aware how modern scholars twist away from the facts. The concept of protection of women has been presented by them as controlling them, and against feminist concept of equality. Result is clear now when the society is not contributing to the prescribed protection of women, and we depend on the government to save women like "Nirbhaya".

Even in comparative terms, daughters were considered equal to son, rather had been considered much more important than sons.

दशपुत्रसमा कन्या दशपुत्रान्प्रवर्धयन् ।

यत्फलं लभते मर्त्यस्तल्लभ्यं कन्ययैकया ॥

A daughter is equal to ten sons in importance, and rearing of one daughter gives parents virtue equal to rearing of ten sons. This is because the ladies are the creators of the future of a nation, as per the below line:

नार्यस्तु राष्ट्रस्य श्र:।

And who cannot see the respect for mothers here:

मातृदेवीम नमस्तुभ्यं मम जन्मदात्रिम त्वम् नमो नम:।

बाल्यकाले मां पालन कृत्वा मातृकाभ्यो त्वम्न माम्यहम।।

I respect and pray My mother, as goddess, I always offer my respect to her who has given me this life and reared me in childhood! In a similar way, I bow towards all women as mothers who have provided knowledge and support to me.

From the above, it is clear that a woman in those times was having great inherent virtues and excellent qualities. She had immense scope of developing her capacities in ancient India. She was not only considered equal to men in status and opportunities, but was respected and supported by all in the society.

Story 4 What one observes

One of its significant attributes of Hinduism is worshiping Ishwara in the feminine form and giving equal status to women in society.

Almost all villages are having Devi Pindi, or places of worship, and the worship of divine women powers in various forms has continued in every state of India. In Hinduism, females and males are the two halves of 'one whole' in the form of *Shiva* and *Shakti*.

The Hindu scriptures sing the prayers extolling the quality of the female divine, highlighting the spiritual equality among male and female deities while accepting the differences in their manifested forms.

In an ideal social tradition, a woman is treated as a princess at her parents' home and a queen by her in-laws. Though at various points in history, the society became patriarchal for various reasons, it never crossed the red line unlike other societies beyond the boundaries of Bharat Varsha.

An Indian woman since her childhood sees that the society does not lampoon her, and never treat her as a second-class citizen. She grows up hearing anecdotes of Mahabharata and Ramayan wherein women are often the central characters.

She never finds that the scriptures promote, propagate and advocate physical or psychological violence against them. At her home she finds that her mother plays a vital and central role in the family decision making process.

An Indian woman sees that Goddess Lakshmi, Durga, Saraswati, Kali are the feminine divine form who are revered and worshipped by millions of Hindus. She finds that the society derives inspiration from the lives of Mother Sita, Mother Yashoda, Draupadi and Kunti. She comes across great saints, queens and several women who actively participated in India's freedom struggle.

So, even an educated woman knows that if Vedic culture were against women, then how did these women, and their mothers gained so much prominence in Indian society and family.

However, a long rule by the foreign powers having the colonial mindset could have instilled the mindset of insecurity, resulting in huge changes in social behavior towards women during the long period of slavery.

Even after independence, we have been enslaved by the western education system. Such education and media have resulted in a very materialistic society, where our basic ideas and culture is getting diminishing importance day by day.

Materialism which has spread its wings has created an idealless and virtue less culture. It instigates people to satisfy their wanton desires by adopting any means. Close scrutiny would reveal that proponents of materialism in fact have no respect for women. In garb of equal rights and status, they use women as a tool to further their business interests.

The rape cases, dowry death, bride burning and other evils which have penetrated the Indian society are because people have given up adhering to the Vedic standards.

Strict laws although can act as a deterrent but still it would not completely eradicate the menace. The thief, the murderer, and all criminal already know the law, yet they still commit violent crimes, due to their materialistic and unclean thoughts. Remedy is only to going back to a society which respects the way of God, the way of its great culture.

So, this third part of the series of books on Puranas is dedicated to the great women of our ancient culture. The purpose is to remember and learn from their lives, and as a society adopt our great culture giving respect, equality and divinity to women.

Even if you do not like learnings and information from your past, the stories of Puranas are important for the high entertainment values provided by them. These are more interesting than modern science fictions.

You have already enjoyed the stories of Puranas from first two parts of series. Some of these stories were about the great goddesses including of Mahamaya being invoked to save Brahma from Madhu and Kaitabh, of Dakshayani becoming Sati in Yagya Kunda, Bhagiratha getting Ganga to leading to the Bharata Bhumi, and of great women like Shakuntala, Madalasa, Urvasi, Sachi, and Maneka in first part of the series.

You have also enjoyed the wonderful stories about birth of Parvati, and her prayers, and marriage with Shiva, and Ganga marrying Shantanu, and becoming mother of Bhishma, marriage of Rukmini with Krishna, and of Rati in the second part of the series.

So, now I invite you for learning and entertainment from this third part of the series on "Stories from Puranas and History."

The stories are about the women Rissikas, sages and great Goddesses.

You will not like to miss any of these stories, whether you are a mature seeker of ancient history and mythology of India, or a reader seeking values with entertainment.

The next chapter is about women-centered hymns from our scriptures, and information from Vedas about the women Rishikas, or Brahmavadini along with the Goddesses of Veda.

CHAPTER 2 HYMNS EULOGIZING WOMEN

In Rigveda, women have been eulogized in general in several Richas. Some Richas equate women to Brahm itself. An example is there in eighth Mandal.

"स्त्री हि ब्रह्मा बभूविथ" (RV 8।33।19) simply means that woman surely is Brahm.

Sachi, a Rissika, says in the tenth Mandal of Rig Veda

अहं केतुरहं मूर्धाऽमुग्रा विवाचिनी।

ममेदनुक्रतुं पतिः सेहानाया उपाचरेत्। (RV 10।159।2)

I am the top knower, I am the highest thinker, I am the best speaker. Following my words and actions, my husband performs every act.

And, in the third Mandal, (RV 3।53।4), a housewife is eulogized as below

जायेदस्तं मधवन्त्सेदु योनि स्तदित्वा युक्ता हरयो वहन्तु॥

Presence and work of a housewife makes a house prosperous. Her presence only makes the house attractive.

Society begins with the pairing of an individual with his or her mate; and for this purpose, the Vedic literature provides for a highly evolved concept of married life. In the Vedic society, the marriage and its philosophy is not an anthropological evolution, from primitivism to the present-day variations and modifications.

The Vedic verses have, from the earliest days been inspiring for a highly evolved concept of family. The Vedic verses have their own characteristic style in laying down these concepts.

One may refer to the Hymn 85 of Book X of the Rigveda (the

same occurring with modification in the Atharva, Book XIV). It explains the marriage of an ideal woman. Savitri Surya is the rissika (or the inspired lady interpreter) of the hymn. Again, Surya is an ideal lady in general who is going to be married.

सम्राज्ञी श्वशुरे भव सम्राज्ञी श्वश्वां भव ।

ननान्दरि सम्राज्ञीं भव सम्राज्ञी अधि देवृषु ॥

samrājñī śvaśure bhava samrājñī śvaśrvām bhava | nanāndari samrājñī bhava samrājñī adhi devṛṣu ||

O newly-wed lady, you enjoy the status of the queen in the house of your in-laws; for your father-in law; your mother-in-law, your sister-in-law and your brother-in-law. (RV 10|85|46)

समंज्ञन्तु विश्वे देवाः समापो हृदयानि नौ ।

सं मांतरिश्वा सं धाता समु देष्ट्री दधातु नौ ॥

sam añjantu viśve devāḥ sam āpo hṛdayāni nau | sam mātariśvā sam dhātā sam u deṣṭrī dadhātu nau ||

Properly enjoined both of us (wife and husband) all divinities, our hearts and and life, and jointly provide us prosperity and progenies. (RV 10|85|47)

There are several hymns in other scriptures also, which have the similar meanings. For example,

"न गृहं गृहमित्याहु:, गृहिणी गृहमुच्यते।"

That house cannot be called a home, in which there is no wife; only when a wife resides, the house becomes home.

In Yajurveda, we find respect for the skill and qualities of women, in such hymns

स्वैर्दक्षेर्दक्षपितेह सीद, देवानाऽसुम्ने बृहते रणाय। -(YV 14|3)

Reside in this house with your skills and your qualities, for enhancing divine qualities and excessive happiness.

Then, let us quote from Atharva Veda also.

प्रति तिष्ठ विराडसि, विष्णुरिवेह सरस्वति।

सिनीवालि प्र जायताँ, भगस्य सुमतावसत्॥ (AV 14|2|15)

O great lady, reside here respectfully! Shining graciously like Saraswati for all! O mother! Reside bearing and rearing great children, and bringing great luck to us.

It is generally held by Western Scholars and their blind followers that widows were Burned with their husband's dead body.

Rigveda or any other shastra does not mention anywhere about the practice of the burning or burial of widows with their dead husbands.

Veda commands the widow to return to her house, to live with her children and grandchildren; and confers on her the right to properties of her deceased husband.

Veda clearly approves marriage of the widow. Such women faced no condemnation or isolation in the household or society. They had the right to property inherited from the dead husbands. There are Richas blessing the woman and her new husband, with progeny and happiness.

A set of 14 Richa in 18th Mandala of the 10th Sukta deal with treatment of widows.

Rigveda (10.18.7) is recited by the dead man's brothers and others, requesting the widow to release her husband's body for cremation.

The Richa also commands the widow to return to the world of living beings, return to her home and to her children and grandchildren.

इमा नारीरविधवाः सुपत्नीराञ्जनेन सर्पिषा सं विशन्तु ।
अनश्रवोऽनमीवाः सुरत्ना आ रोहन्तु जनयो योनिमग्रे ॥

imā nārīr avidhavāḥ supatnīr āñjanena sarpiṣā saṁ viśantu |
anaśravo namīvāḥ suratnā ā rohantu janayo yonim agre ||

Rigveda not only sanctions survival of a widow and her right to property; but also approves her marriage with the brother of her dead husband; and to live with full dignity and honor in the family.

उदीर्ष्व नार्यभि जीवलोकं गतासुमेतमुप शेष एहि ।
हस्तग्राभस्य दिधिषोस्तवेदं पत्युर्जनित्वमभि सं बभूथ ॥

ud īrṣva nāry abhi jīvalokaṁ gatāsum etam upa śeṣa ehi |
hastagrābhasya didhiṣos tavedaṁ patyur janitvam abhi sam babhūtha ||

Go up, O woman, to the world of living; you stand by this one who is deceased; come! to him who grasps your hand, your second spouse (didhisu), you have now entered into the relation of wife to husband.

This Vedic Verse also, confers upon her full right on house and properties of her deceased husband.

In **Rigveda (10.18.9)** the new husband while taking the widow as his wife says to her:

धनुर्हस्तादाददानो मृतस्यास्मे क्षत्राय वर्चसे बलाय ।
अत्रैव त्वमिह वयं सुवीरा विश्वाः स्पृधौ अभिमातीर्जयेम ॥

dhanur hastād ādadāno mṛtasyāsme kṣatrāya varcase balāya |
atraiva tvam iha vayaṁ suvīrā viśvāḥ spṛdho abhimātīr jayema ||

"let us launch a new life of valor and strength taking the reign of bow and arrow in our hands controlling the rule of law in this house, begetting male children overcoming all enemies who may assail us."

Similarly, **Atharv Veda (18-3-4)** blesses the widow to have a happy life with present husband:

प्रंजानत्य□घ्ये जीवलोकं देवानां पन्थांमनुसंचरंती।
अयं तेगोर्पतिस्तं जुषस्व स्वर्गं लोकमधिं रोहयैनम् ॥

O never punishable one! (the widow) tread the path of wise in front of thee and choose this man (another suitor) as thy husband. Joyfully receive him and may the two of you mount the world of happiness.

Rigveda reveals a tolerant and moderately unbiased society characterized by sanctity of the institution of marriage, domestic purity and women and high honor for women.

The women did receive a fair and an equitable treatment and they were empowered to deal with issues that mattered in the life around them.

Similar expressions of respect and equality are observed in Brahmanas. Taittariya Brahmana states that woman is half part of everyone.

अर्धौ वा एष आत्मनः यत पत्नी। (TB 3।3।3।5).

It says further that every great work, Yagya is incomplete if not performed with wife.

अयज्ञो वा एषः। योऽपत्नीकः। (TB 2।2।2।6।)

Aitreya Brahmana equals Wife to the household fire, saying

जाया गार्हपत्यः (AB 8.24).

Śatpatha Brahmana specifically forbids disrespect of women.

न वै स्त्रियं हन्ति। (SB 11.4.3.2)

Taittariya Brahmana says that the woman is Shri or Laxmi herself,

"श्रिया वाएतद् रुप्यं यत् पत्नयः।" (TB 3.9.4.7)

In Upanishads, nowhere is any difference between creations of God. As such, equal treatment of man and woman cannot be questioned.

यः सर्वेषु भूतेषु तिष्ठन्सर्वेभ्यो भूतेभ्योऽन्तरो

यं सर्वाणि भूतानि न विदुर्यस्य सर्वाणि भूतानि शरीरं

यः सर्वाणि भूतान्यन्तरो यमयत्येष त आत्मान्त्याभ्यमृतः।

(Brihadaranyaka U 3।7।15)

Who resides in every creation, inside him/her/it, controls it's body and functioning without being known, know that to be your Soul, Atma.

Among other scriptures, Brihatsamhita states,

"पुरुषाणाँ सहस्रं च सती स्त्री समुद्धरेत्।"

meaning that a pious woman can lead thousands of persons to progress and development.

Vyas Samhita has an interesting hymn

"यायन्त विन्दते जायाँ, तावदर्धोभवेतपुमान्".

This means that a man is incomplete unless he is married.

Let us now examine the Puranas as well. Story of Goddesses are in several Puranas, including Shiva Purana, Brahmanda Purana, Brahmvaivart Purana, Shrimad Bhagavata Purana, Devi Bhagavat Purana and Markandeya Purana. Let me quote a wonderful hymn from Markandeya Purana:

विद्या समस्तास्तव देवि भेदाः।

स्त्रियः समस्ता सकला जगत्सु॥,

which says that the Goddess is in all the forms of knowledge and also all the women in the world.

This surely shows the respect towards women in Puranic times.

Besides the stories of Goddesses, we read stories of many great women in Puranas.

Next, we find the books on Tantra Shastra. Undoubtedly, the Tantra shastras are full of devotion, respect and prayers towards women. The hymns are full of such lines as given below from Tara Khanda of Shakti Agam Tantra:

नारी त्रैलोक्य जननी, नारी त्रैलोक्य रुपिणी।
नारी त्रिभुवनादारा, नारी शक्ति स्वरुपिणी॥ (Tarakhanda 13.44)

Women are mothers of all the inhabitants of all three Lokas, they are actually all Lokas, and are the energy of all the three Lokas. There are several similar lines are in the book eulogizing women, as follows:

न च नारी समं सौख्यं, न च नारी समागति,
न च नारी सदृषं भाग्यं, न च भूतो न भविष्यति।
न च नारी सदृषं राज्यं, न च नारी सदृषं तप:,
 न च नारी सदृषं तीर्थं, न भूतं न भविष्यति। (13.46)
न नारी सदृषो योगो, न नारी सदृषो जप:,
 न नारी सदृषो योगो, न भूतो न भविष्यति।
न नारी सदृषो मन्त्र:, न नारी सदृषं तप:,
न नारी सदृषं वित्तं, न भूतो न भविष्यति। - (13.48)

This says that a woman is the best. There is no bliss, no status, no luck like her. It never happened and will never be so. Similarly, no sovereignty, no Tapasya, no Tirth, no Yoga, no Japa, no mantra, no property equal to her, neither in past, not in present and never in future.

CHAPTER 3: RISHIKA, AND BRAHMAVADINIS

Story 1: Rishika of Vedas

There was a very prevalent thinking during start of the nineteenth century that women cannot read Vedas and should not pray through Gayatri Mantra. Even today, several so-called Pandits accept such superstitious thought, and even preach that they should not do so.

This is the case while they fully accept the fact that women are more prominent in respect of virtues like chastity, loyalty, compassion, service, sympathy, love affection, generosity and devotion. Most of the Vrata and prayers are performed by women only.

I this respect, we should explore the contribution of women towards ancient scriptures. It is obvious from the records that there were a number of Rishikas and Brahmvadinis in ancient times.

Vedic literature is considered as the sacred source of final authority in Hinduism. These are held to be eternal and called "Shruti" or, "that which has been heard", or received through revelation. If we examine the Vedas, we know that the hymns are not prayers, but the knowledge realized by great sages.

The *Rig Veda* is a collection of Richas, the hymns which explore and explain the Rits. These Rits are the true information, or true laws obeyed by material, human, and divine elements. The individual cosmic true rules, or Rits followed by different elements of nature have been described in these Richas of Rig Veda. Then, there are Richas describing different true rules, Rits to be followed by humans.

There was no gender bias in those days when God revealed the Vedas to sages. We observe that the divine truth was realized not only by male but also by female sages or Rishika. If we examine the Richas of the Rig Veda, we observe that not only Rishis, but several wives of these rishis were also seers to whom Rigvedic Richas were revealed.

In Nirukt, a Rishi is defined as one who is a seer of Mantras, or Richa, who understand the secret meaning of the same, and is able to transmit the meaning and secret of Richas to others.

As per Vrihad Devta, out of over 414 rishis, twenty-nine are ladies. Presence of Rishika implies gender equality. How could the great God, who is just and impartial, discriminate between man and woman, who are both his children.

Presence of so many Rishika in Rigveda proves that Almighty God Himself considered woman fit enough, qualified and eligible to receive divine revelations. Therefore, women had equal claim over the Vedas. Women were neither discriminated in matters of religion and education nor were prevented from gaining excellence in the society.

Vedas thus speak of this type of gender equality. They do not discriminate against women. If God Himself did not discriminate women in matters of religion, then how could any else or we at the society level?

Important and famous Rishika of rig Veda are Ghosha, Godha, Vishvavara, Aapala, Upnishad, Juhu, Adity, Indrani, Sarama, Romasha, Urvashi, Lopamudra, Yami, Shasvati, Suryaa, Savitri, Vagambhrini. They were also called Brahmavadini, since they were able to explain the Brahm to all.

The most famous Rigveda Suktas revealed to these Brahmavadinis are 10-39, 10-40, 10-85, 10-91, 10-95, 10-107, 10-109, 10-125, 10-134, 10-154, 10-159, 10-189, 5-28, 8-91, and others.

Story 2: Brahmana scriptures and Grihya and shrouta sutras

As per Brahmana Granthas, there are ample evidence of females performing Yagya like the male. Several Yagya required presence of both wife and husband as Yajmana. Moreover, there were women hotas, expert in Yagya techniques and religious knowledge.

The learned women guided their fathers, or husbands in Yagya techniques.It is stated that Ida had told her father Manu that she would do avadhan, or Home on fire in such a way that he would attain all worldly riches.

Ashvalaya Grihya Sutra provides that in the absence of a male head, his wife, son, or unmarried daughter could perform Yagya. Shatpatha Brahmana has directions for women about pronouncing Mantras of Yajurved. Same is the case with mantras of Taittariya Upanishad.

While performing Samajjan as per Vivah shukta (10-85) of RigVeda, both the bride and the groom are required to chant the Richa (10-85-48). As prescribed in Paraskar Grahya Sutra, the bride is required to hymns of Laja Hom at the time of marriage, and to chant Yajurved mantra while meditating on the sun.

Tandya Brahmana directs women to play on Veena and sing Sam in the battle. It also directs to keep a pitcher on the head and to sing the Sam hymns.

In other Shrout sutras also, there are clear directions about chanting of Veda hymns and Sam mantras with rhythm. There are clear directions that unmarried girls should also chant hymns of Vedas.

Story 3: Brahmavadinis from Upanishads

The Upanishads were a part of the later Vedic texts. The Upanishadic thinkers were men especially Brahmins and rajas. However, there were exceptions as well and we find some very famous women sages.

Gargi and Maitreyi were two famous women thinkers of the Upanishads.

Gargi was a woman Upanishadic thinker who was known for her learning. She participated in debates held in royal courts.

Maitreyi was a representative individual of women during the Vedic period. She prayed to her husband to tell her the way to the path of immortality.

She was known for her contributions to the Vedas and her role in breaking down gender barriers in ancient Indian society. She was also a Brahmavadini.

We may discuss the roles of these Brahmavadinis in next

chapters separately.

Other famous women who appeared in the Upanishads include Jabala, the unwed mother of great sage Satyakam, and the wife of Satyakam Jabala. They are being mentioned to understand the plight of women who may be considered very ordinary in all ages, in ancient India.

As per Story of Satyakam Brahm Vidya, when Satyakam wanted to go to gurukul, he asked his mother Jabala the name of his father for applying for admission.

Jabala was not a married woman. But she was truthful. She said to him, "I do not know, my child of what family you belong to. I obtained you when, in my youth, I attended upon many persons, and devoted to their service. So, I do not know of what family you are. But I am *Jabala* by name and you are *Satyakam* by name and you are my son. So, you may declare yourself as *Satyakam Jabala.*"

This was what was told by Satyakam when he was asked about his family by the sage Gautama-Haridrumata before admitting him for education.

Happy with his truthfulness, Gautama accepted him as his disciple. Satyakam was thereafter known by Satyakam Jabala, perhaps the first person in the world to be known by his mother's name.

Satyakam Jabala became very famous scholar and teacher. We hear of Satyakam Jabala's wife in the story of Agni Brahm Vidya. Upakosala, one of the very sincere disciples of Satyakam Jabala was not declared successful by him even after completion of required period of study. Here, we find the wife of teacher caring for the student as a mother.

Respect for all women is crystal clear from these instances.

Story 4: Other great women

We are acquainted with stories of several other highly learned and spiritually illumined women of ancient India, such as Madalasa, Anusuya, Arundhati, Ahilya, Devayani, Kunti, Shatrupa, Vrinda, Tara, Draupadi, Savitri, Mandodari, Shakuntala, Vaishalini, Parvati, Satyavati, Sita, Gandhari, and others.

They had elevated their souls and attained Yoga siddhis through their study, and Tapasya. We have learned about several of these great ladies from first and second part of "Stories from Puranas," and will read in this book also.

All those who have studied ancient Indian histories and scriptures know it well that all the aforesaid women and others were unparalleled shining stars in their own rights. Their stories are examples of virtues like knowledge, learning, energy, courage, devotion, morality, spiritual awakening, and excellence in their spiritual and mental attainments.

We will read the story of Savitri, and Vedavathi in this book later, who performed Tapasya for a long period. Savitri was able to bring back her husband, Satyavan, from Yama. We have already read in previous part of the series, the story of Sukanya, whose penance was successful in transforming his old husband to a beautiful young person.

In the book Shankar Digvijaya (3/16), we find a mention of one Bharati Devi, who had challenged Adi Shankaracharya for debate. She was well-versed in all the Vedas and other scriptures and even other branches of knowledge. During the debate, her exposition of the scriptures was so marvelous that even eminent scholars were wonder-struck. Shankaracharya had to seek one months' time to respond to her profound questions.

So, at least up to the time of control of Muslims, there was no such partial thought of women not being permitted to study Vedas and ancient scriptures.

Even later, in the areas controlled by Hindu kings, there was no such thinking. We know that queen Ahilya Bai a very learned lady, who had ruled her people very well. She was a very virtuous lady, and had renovated the temples of Vishnupad in Gaya, and temples in Varanasi, Mathura, and other places. There are several such examples.

Story 5: Story of Kumari Kalyani

However, several evil orthodox traditions and conventions became prevalent in Middle Ages, particularly in the areas ruled by Muslim kings. The scholars of Kashi were of the opinion that women do not have the right to chant Ved Mantras. So, a reformist movement was required to admit one girl student for a Veda course.

A girl named Kumari Kalyani was proficient in Sanskrit and the knowledge of scriptures. She wanted to get admission to a course in which Vedas were taught in Banaras Hindu University. She was refused admission to the course.

The authorities were following the prevalent belief that a woman, according to Shastras, had no right to chant Ved Mantras. But, the girl student represented again and again showing that there is no prohibition by any Shastra.

The controversy continued for some time. On of the local paper "Sarvadeshik" publishes several articles in support of the right of women to study and chant Ved Mantras, while the paper "Siddhanta" took the other side, and refuted the claim. A deputation of Arya Samaj met the University authorities, and there was a prolonged discussion on the subject.

Ultimately, Banaras Hindu University decided to appoint a committee of Vedic scholars headed by Mahamana Madan Mohan Malviya. The committee, after a thorough study of the shastras, gave the decision that women have the same right as men. They may not be denied to study Veda.

Malviya ji announced this decision of committee on 22nd August 1946. Kumari Kalyani was admitted, and she opened the gate of study of Vedas for all women.

CHAPTER 4: GODDESSES IN VEDAS AND UPANISHADS

Story 1: Goddesses in Vedas
Vedas are the first Hindu scriptures that contain a collection of hymns celebrating deities, or divine powers representing different aspects of Ishwar. From these, we get the names of deities, both Gods and Goddesses. It is important to note that one of these deities have been given any specific mythological or historical roles, or focus in the Rig Veda.

Rigveda, one of the oldest sacred texts of Hinduism, features innumerable deities, including several prominent goddesses. However, some deities have dominated as a subject of description in Rig Veda. As per the number of Richas describing the Rits or properties linked with the divine power, we find Agni, Soma, Indra, Ashwini duo as most important deities.

Then, there are several Richas describing other male deities including Varuna, Mitra, Surya, Vayu, Vishwakarma and others. However, Richas of Rig Veda also narrate the feminine divine powers representing Ishwar.

The first mentioned Goddess in Rig Veda is Sarasvati. She and other Goddess Usa have been described in more Richas than the second ranked male deities. Other important women deities in Rig Veda are Ratri, Aditi, Vagdevi, Prithvi, Nirrti, Surya, and Sachi.

It is pointed out by some scholars that number of female deities and Richas describing them are much lower than the male deities. However, it must be remembered that Rig Veda describes all deities as different aspects of one Ishwara, while mentioning them mostly as a natural phenomenon, or divine powers. And the God is one.

All these female deities represent essential aspects of life, nature, and the cosmic status. The hymns dedicated to them reflect the reverence for feminine principles within the broader context of Vedic spirituality and cosmology.

We may discuss individually the most important goddesses, which are Sarasvati, Vak devi, Usha and Ratri, Aditi, and Prithvi. Although Gayatri Mantra is mentioned in three richas of Rig Veda, later scriptures have detailed the goddess a lot. So, one chapter will be dedicated to Gayatri as well.

Other goddesses like Nrriti, Raka, Sinivali, Parendi, Puramdhi, Suryaa, Danu, Saranyu, Aranyani, and Sarama have been referred in more Richas in Rig Veda, but they have little mention in later scriptures. So, we are not narrating their role individually.

Story 2: Goddesses in Upanishads

If we explore major Upanishads, there is even less importance given here to individual deities.

Upanishads do not provide detailed stories of Gods and Goddesses. The Brahm explored by sages and teachers in Upanishads is without any shape or form or gender.

The Brahm or Atma discussed in Brahm Vidyas, the wisdom from Upanishads is neither masculine, nor feminine. Actually, it denotes all animate creatures and also inanimate ones. So, Brahm may be considered as masculine, feminine, neutral, or both.

As you might have observed in Brahm Vidyas, the pearls of wisdom selected from Upanishads, the concept of Purusha is given in most of the Brahma Vidyas.

Purusha is that which resides in 'पुर' or body of an animate or inanimate and fills it completely 'पुर एती'. It controls the person without being known to him/her/it in whose body it resides.

As per Madhu Brahm Vidya from fifth Brahm of Brihadaranyaka Upanishad (refer my book Madhu Vidya: Straight from Horse's

Mouth), Brahm or Atma is expressed as Purusha, and described as follows:

सर्वेषाम भूतानाम राजा

It is the emperor of all beings-everything and everybody.

Everything is controlled by the very existence and presence of this atman, without any movement on Its part. As the spokes are connected to the hub of a wheel, everything visible or invisible is connected to and ruled by this atman. All beings, whatever can be conceived of or not conceived of, all divine powers, all the worlds that can be conceived of and are in any level of manifestation, everything that is vital and real, everything, all beings, whatever is, in any form, are properly fixed to, linked with this atman, in the same way as every spoke is with the hub of the wheel.

पुरश्चक्रे द्विपदः पुरश्चक्रे चतुष्पदः ।

puraś cakre dvipadaḥ, puraś cakre catuṣpadaḥ.

पुरः स पक्षी भूत्वा

puraḥ sa pakṣī bhūtvā

पुरः पुरुष आविशदती । puraḥ puruṣa āviśat iti.

स वा अयं पुरुषः सर्वासु पूर्षु पुरीशयो

sa vā ayam puruṣaḥ sarvāsu pūrsu puriśayaḥ,

नैनेन किंचिनानावृतम

nainena kiṁ ca nānāvṛtam,

नैनेन किंचिनासंवृतम ॥ १८ ॥

nainena kiṁ ca nāsaṁvṛtam.

This Being which is responsible for the interconnectedness of things has become, what you call, the living and the non-living; the visible and the invisible; the creatures which are two footed and those that are four-footed.

He became the subtle body and then the gross body by means of a subtle instrument known as the Linga body or Sukshma body. The very Being became the vital consciousness of all physical bodies, and He is present in everybody. The Body that is Universal and the body that is particularized – there is nothing that it is not enveloping.

Everything is covered up by That – idaṁ sarvam."

अयमात्मा ब्रह्म सर्वानुभू ॥ इति अनुशासनम ॥

ayam ātmā brahma sarvānubhūḥ, ity anuśāsanam.

This self, the perceiver of everything, is Brahman. This is the teaching.

Different attributes of Brahma like it being Akshara, it being Bhuma, it residing in small fort of heart, and others are described in different Brahm Vidyas.

The identification of Brahm as masculine, as well as feminine, and neutral genders is specifically provided in Paryanka Brahm vidya. As per the Brahm Vidya, when the Atma fulfilling all requirement, and passing through all gates reaches the Brahma sitting on his Paryanka (cozy seat), Brahma asks,

"तमाह केन पौंस्रानि नामान्याप्नोतीति प्राणेनेति ब्रूयात्केन

स्त्रीनामानीति वाचेति केन नपुंसकनामानीति मनसेति केन ."

Brahma asks to Atma, "By what means did you obtain my masculine names?"

He should say to him, "By Prana, breath."

" By what means, you identified my feminine names"

"By Vak, speech."

"By what (did you obtain) my neutral names?'

"By my mind"

Only after knowing that there is no difference in Atma and Brahm, one attains Advait with Brahm.

This Brahm Vidya has been narrated in detail in second part of my series of books on "Eternal Meditation Principles: Brahm Vidyas"

Similarly, all thirty-two Brahm Vidyas, or the pearls of wisdom identified from Upanishads leading to Brahm are not having specific Gods or Goddesses. These are fully covered in my three-book series on "Eternal Meditation Principles: Brahm Vidya."

While some Brahma Vidyas are describing Agni, or Surya, or Vaisvanara, it is important to note that all indicate the Purusha, or Brahma. So, we need not search for different gods and goddesses in Upanishads.

However, there are short introductory stories about Sri, Laxmi,

Saraswati, Durga, and other Goddesses in various Upanishads, which take complete shape in the stories of Puranas.

We also know several Shakta Upanishads individually glorifying Goddesses, such as Sita Upanishad, Radha Upanishad, Kalika Upanishad, and others.

We will narrate them along with the stories from Puranas. We are also selecting one pearl of wisdom from Upanishads glorifying Gayatri from Upanishads, and will narrate it separately.

The story of Ken Upanishad describing the Goddess Uma Haimavati may be considered a nice example of some stories of Goddesses from Upanishads.

It is in the third part of the Upanishad.

Brahm, according to the story, obtained a victory for the gods; and by that victory of Brahman the gods became elated. They said to themselves: "Verily, this victory is ours; verily, this glory is ours only."

Brahm, to be sure, understood it all and appeared before them. But they did not know who that adorable Spirit was.

They said to Agni (Fire): "O Agni! Find out who this great Spirit is."

"Yes," he said and hastened to It.

Brahm asked him: "Who are you?"

He replied: "I am known as Agni; I am also called Jataveda."

Brahm said: "What power is in you, who are so well known?"

Fire replied: "I can burn all— whatever there is on earth." Brahm put a straw before him and said: "Burn this."

He rushed toward it with all his power, but could not burn it. Then he returned from the Spirit and said to the gods: "I could not find out who this Spirit is,"

Then they said to Vayu (Air), "O Vayu! Find out who this great Spirit is."

"Yes," he said and hastened to It.

Brahm asked him: "Who are you?"

He replied "I am known as Vayu."

Brahm said: "What power is in you, who are so well known?"

Vayu replied: "I can carry off all— whatever there is on earth." Brahm put a straw before him and said: "Carry this."

He rushed toward it with all his strength, but could not move it. Then he returned from the Spirit and said to the gods: "I could not find out who this Spirit is,"

Then the gods said to Indra: "O Maghavan! Find out who this great Spirit is."

"Yes," he said and hastened to It.

But the Spirit disappeared from him. Then Indra beheld in that very region of the sky a Woman highly adorned. She was Uma, the daughter of the Himalayas.

He approached Her and said, "Who is this great Spirit?"

She replied: "It is, indeed, Brahman. Through the victory of Brahman alone have you attained glory."

After that Indra understood that It was Brahm, who was the real power behind their victory.

We are selecting two of the Rishika from Upanishads, and narrate their stories in next two chapters.

CHAPTER 5 GARGI VACHAKNAVI

Story 1 Introduction

Gargi was the daughter of the sage Vachaknu from the lineage of the sage Garga (c. 800-500 BCE), and was hence named after her father. From a young age, Vachaknavi was very intellectual, acquiring knowledge of the Vedas and scriptures. She remained celibate throughout her life.

She was as knowledgeable in Vedas and Upanishads as the best scholars of the Vedic times and could very well contest the male-philosophers in debates. Her name appears in the Grahya Sutras of Asvalayana. She was a leading scholar who also made rich contributions to propagate education.

She is very well Known for her contributions, including

1. **Brahmavadini**

Gargi was known as Brahmavadini, which means she had knowledge of Brahma Vidya.

2. **Vedic scriptures**

She was a renowned expounder of the Vedas. Gargi, as Brahmavadini, composed several hymns in the Rigveda (in X 39. V.28) that questioned the origin of all existence.

3. **Intellectual debates**

She participated in public debates and intellectual discussions with other philosophers.

4. **Brahma yajna**

She debated the sage Yajnavalkya at a philosophic debate organized by King Janaka of Videha.

Story 2: Akshar Brahm Vidya:
The famous debate between Gargi and Yajnavalkya in the assembly of religious discussions called by the King Janaka is well known among the readers of Upanishads. The pearl of wisdom received from this discussion is famous as the Akshara Brahm Vidya.

This Brahm Vidya is discussed in detail in my book "Eternal Meditation Principles: Brahm Vidyas Part 1."
It is presented in brief below:

Brahm Yagya
King Janaka was a great knower of the Self. He wanted to know who was the most learned in his country, to make him/ her his guru. He arranged a great Yagya. During the Yagya, he announced a great reward for the best of knower.

When Janak asked "Great men, learned people. Who is the greatest knower of Truth among you?" None of them was bold enough to come forward. Everybody kept quiet. But, Yajnavalkya, the great Master, was in that assembly. He came forward to take the reward.

Now, other scholars present in the Yagya were not happy. They challenged him. In this way, number of great discussions started. The detail discussions are narrated from fourth Brahmana to tenth Brahmana of Brihadaranyaka Upanishad, and introduce us to several Brahm Vidyas.

Yajnavalkya was able to answer the serious questions asked by scholars such as Asvala, the chief priest of Mithila, Ushasta, and Kahola Kausitakeya, when Gargi challenged with her questions. She asked question pertaining to the various realms of existence, the different worlds which succeed, one after another, in different degrees of density, the succeeding ones pervading the preceding ones and being larger in extent than them; ultimately, the highest pervading principle being regarded as Prajapati Hiranyagarbha. She was stopped to ask further as beyond Prajapati, there can be nothing conceivably more pervasive, higher realm of existence.

Then Gargi got down and occupied her seat and sat quite for other scholars to ask their questions. Then Yajnavalkya satisfied next scholar Aruni expounding the Antaryamin Brahm Vidya.

Discussion leading to Akshar Vidya

After this session, Gargi stood up and again challenged Yajnavalkya to answer her two questions, which she compared with two sharp arrows. She declared to all scholars, "There is no use arguing with him afterwards, if he is capable of answering these two questions."

These two questions are famous for their philosophical depths:

सा होवाच यदूर्ध्वं याज्ञवल्क्य दिवो यदवाक्पृथिव्या यदन्तरा
द्यावापृथिवी इमे यद्भूतं च भवच्च भविष्यच्चेत्याचक्षते
कस्मिँस्तदोतं च प्रोतं चेति ॥ ३॥

Now, Gargi speaks "Yajnavalkya; that which is above the heaven; that which is inside the earth; that which is between the earth and the heaven; that which is identical with whatever was, identical with whatever is and also identical with whatever will be; in what is this peculiar thing rooted and founded?"

Actually, while answering the previous scholar, Yajnavalkya had propounded the existence of such an Antaryamin.

So, Gargi asked " If there is something like that, on what is it founded as if there is a support to it ?"

स होवाच यदूर्ध्वं गार्गि दिवो यदवाक्पृथिव्या यदन्तरा
द्यावापृथिवी इमे यद्भूतं च भवच्च भविष्यच्चेत्याचक्षत
आकाशे तदोतं च प्रोतं चेति ॥ ४॥

Then Yajnavalkya replied, "Gargi! This is strung in Akasha, a subtle ethereal principle. That ethereal principle has not the distinction of pervasion of objects. It is subtler than that which pervades it. And that is rooted in some undifferentiated something. That undifferentiated reality can be designated as ether. It is an unmanifest ether 'Avyakrita akasha' not the physical ether."

Gargi was satisfied with this answer. Soon, she followed for the answer of the second part of the question. Now, what Yajnavalkya answered, is famous as Akshara Brahm Vidya.

He told, "The foundation of this substance, which is above and below and between and it is the past, present and future, is nothing but the Absolute. Beyond that, there can be nothing. That is the immaculate Absolute, which is imperishable, or Akshara."

"It is neither gross, nor subtle. Neither long, nor short. It has no colour. It does not cast shadow, and so no light. But it is also brightest of all. It has no organ, no breathe. But it is most alive. It is not inside, not outside, but it exists in every point. It has no want, and is wanted by none. Does not consume, and is also not consumed by anyone. It is no object, but also everything."

Yajnavalkya continued, "By the command of this Akshara, everything functions in this world, O Gargi. It is not a command like that of a boss, by word of mouth, or even by gesture. Its command is merely its Existence. It merely is, and orders by the very Being that it is."

"There is a great mystery and order that we can observe in the workings of the world. The method which is adopted by all the functions of nature seems to be following a sort of law which cannot be violated, is so precise, so exact to the point of logical perfection, that their existence is incomprehensible without assuming the presence of an integrating Power."

"The goal of life is therefore the realisation of this Supreme Being, and every other activity is an auxiliary to this realisation. It is not ultimate in a temporal or spatial sense. It is ultimate in a logical sense only."

Yajnavalkya continued, "But Gargi; this great wonder, the Akshar, about which I am speaking to you cannot be seen by anybody. This Imperishable Absolute is the Seer of everything, but you cannot see It."

"How can you see It? By becoming It. How can you become It? By assimilating Its character. What is Its character? Non-objectivity. It is a tremendous blow to the mind even to conceive what non-objectivity is."

"It is the Hearer of everything, but you cannot hear it. It is the Thinker of everything, but it itself cannot be thought by anybody. It understands everything, but you cannot understand it. You cannot understand it because it is the Cause and you are the effect. It understands everything because it is the Cause of everything and everything is its effect."

"The unmanifested "Avyakrita akasha," the ether supreme, is woven warp and woof, lengthwise and breadthwise, in this Eternal Absolute. Everything is woven in it. You will find even the least of things there, even the minutest and the most insignificant of things can be found in that Supreme Eternal Absolute."

This was a wonderful explanation of the Akshara Brahm. Gargi, after having listened to this reply, this discourse of Yajnavalkya, was fully satisfied of the greatness of wisdom of Yajnavalkya.

She declared to the whole audience, "Friends! Learned men! There is no use of asking him further. We should not put any more questions. You must regard yourself blessed if you can be let off by him merely by a salute."

Story 3 Other Achievements

After this Brahm Yagya, Gargi was honored as one of the Navaratnam (nine gems) in the court of King Janaka of Mithila.

One of the most important books on Yoga, "Yoga Yajnavalkya Book" is also attributed to Gargi along with Yajnavalkya.

This classical text on Yoga, is written as a dialogue between Gargi and the sage Yajnavalkya.

The presence of Gargi in Yoga Yajnavalkya is significant in a historical sense, as encouraging yoga to women. The book includes some yoga-related verses exclusively addressed to women, such as those in verses.

CHAPTER 6: SULABHA MAITREYI

Story 1: Introduction

Maitreyi was a great Indian philosopher and sage who lived in ancient India during the Vedic period. She was born in Mithila in Eastern India to Rishi Maitri. Her father, who lived in the Kingdom of the Videha, Mithila, was a minister in the court of King Janaka.

In per the Asvalayana Gṛhyasutra, the daughter of the sage Maitri is referred to as Sulabha Maitreyi and is mentioned with several other women scholars of the Vedic era.

She was thus called a *brahmavadini* (a female expounder of the *Veda*).

As per Mahabharata, Sulabha Maitreyi was a young beauty who never married. She explained Advaita philosophy (monism) to Janaka and is described as a lifelong ascetic by Mahabharata.

On the other hand, Maitreyi of ancient India, described as an Advaita philosopher, is said to be a wife of the sage Yajnavalkya in the Brihadaranyaka Upanishad in the time of Janaka.

In the Brihadaranyaka Upanishad, Maitreyi is described as scholarly wife of Yajnavalkya. His other wife, Katyayani, was a housewife.

While Yajnavalkya and Katyayani lived in contented domesticity, Maitreyi studied metaphysics and engaged in theological dialogues with her husband in addition to "making self-inquiries of introspection".

She was the niece of Rishi Gargi. She was a devoted disciple of Yajnavalkya, and one of his wives. She chose the path to immortality over her husband's wealth.

She is considered a symbol of Indian intellectual women. She is known for her contributions to the Vedas and her role in breaking down gender barriers in ancient Indian society.

Maitreyi, who is also mentioned in a number of Puranas, "is regarded as one of the most learned and virtuous women of ancient India" and symbolizes intellectual women in India.

She is highly respected for:

1. Contributions to the Vedas

Maitreyi is known as a Brahmavadini, or "speaker of the Brahmana". She wrote ten hymns for the Rig Veda.

2. Dialogue with Yajnavalkya

Maitreyi is known for her dialogue with the sage Yajnavalkya in the Brihadaranyaka Upanishad. In this dialogue, she explores the nature of Atman (soul or self) and Brahman (Supreme Consciousness).

3. Breaking down gender barriers

Maitreyi's dialogue with Yajnavalkya is considered a challenge to the idea that women were only fit to be mothers or wives only.

Story 2: Maitreyi Brahm Vidya

The pearl of wisdom available to us from the discussion between husband and wife is famous as Maitreyi Brahm Vidya. This Brahm Vidya is discussed in detail in my book "Eternal Meditation Principles: Brahm Vidya Part 2."

We give a brief narration below:

The great scholar Yajnavalkya informs Maitreyi, "I plan to retire from the life of a householder soon. Therefore, I desire to arrange the division of property between both of my consorts, you and Katayani before taking to the life of renunciation."

But the idea of property immediately stirred up a brainwave in the mind of the wise Maitreyi.

She questions, "You want to go for Vanaprastha Ashram, and so divide the property between the two of us here, to make us comfortable and happy. If I am the owner of the entire earth along with the wealth of the whole world, will I be perpetually happy?"

"No," replies Yajnavalkya, " The wealth cannot make you happy for ever, but it will make your life very comfortable."

Maitreyi replied, "What am I to do with such thing which is not going to make me perpetually happy, immortal, satisfied? Whatever you know in this context, O Lord, tell me that."

Yajnavalkya was highly pleased and answered, "I never expected that you, my dear, will ask this when I am leaving you immense property. So, I speak the truth. Anything that gives us comfort, physical and social, can be regarded as wealth. But it's presence and value are conditioned by time, impacted by temporality."

He then explained the notion with explanation of Love.

स होवाच न वा अरे पत्युः कामाय पतिः प्रियो भवत्य्
आत्मनस्तु कामाय पतिः प्रियो भवति ।
न वा अरे जायायै कामाय जाया प्रिया भवत्य्
आत्मनस्तु कामाय जाया प्रिया भवति ।
न वा अरे पुत्राणां कामाय पुत्राः प्रिया भवन्त्य्
आत्मनस्तु कामाय पुत्राः प्रिया भवन्ति ।
न वा अरे वित्तस्य कामाय वित्तं प्रियं भवत्य्
आत्मनस्तु कामाय वित्तं प्रियं भवति ।
न वा अरे ब्रह्मणः कामाय ब्रह्म प्रियं भवत्य्
आत्मनस्तु कामाय ब्रह्म प्रियं भवति ।
न वा अरे क्षत्रस्य कामाय क्षत्रं प्रियं भवत्य्
आत्मनस्तु कामाय क्षत्रं प्रियं भवति ।
न वा अरे लोकानां कामाय लोकाः प्रिया भवन्त्य्
आत्मनस्तु कामाय लोकाः प्रिया भवन्ति ।
न वा अरे देवानां कामाय देवाः प्रिया भवन्त्य्
आत्मनस्तु कामाय देवाः प्रिया भवन्ति ।
न वा अरे भूतानां कामाय भूतानि प्रियाणि भवन्त्य्
आत्मनस्तु कामाय भूतानि प्रियाणि भवन्ति ।
न वा अरे सर्वस्य कामाय सर्वं प्रियं भवत्य्
आत्मनस्तु कामाय सर्वं प्रियं भवत्य्

आत्मा वा अरे द्रष्टव्यः श्रोतव्यो मन्तव्यो निदिध्यासितव्यो ।
निदिध्यासितव्यस् मैत्रेय्य् आत्मनो वा अरे दर्शनेन
श्रवणेन मत्या विज्ञानेनेदꣳ सर्वं विदितम् ॥ ५ ॥

Yajnavalkya says, " The husband is dear to the wife not for his sake, but for her own sake. Similarly, the wife is dear to the husband not for her sake, but for his own sake. He or She becomes dear for the sake of your own soul, to attain a condition which your soul imagines to be available through that relation with your husband or wife."

"Similarly, son or wealth or knowledge, etc. are not dear or lovable or desirable to you because of their sake. It is something else that your soul loves and desires to fulfil through its occupation. But you have a completely misconstrued belief that you love the object."

"What you love is only the condition that you imagine to be present in the state of the possession of the object, or that relationship."

Yajnavalkya goes on with his exposition to Maitryi, "That assumed condition is always missed, remains a mirage, and so the happiness expected never comes."

"For the desire of the Self, anything appears to be desirable. For the sake of attaining the Supreme Absolute, Selfhood of all beings, you are unknowingly asking for 'things' external to you. It is a wild goose chase from birth to death, nothing coming forth, ultimately."

"You come to this world crying, and you go crying, because you have missed the real issue. It is the Atman that is to be beheld; it is the atman that is to be known; it is the atman which is to be meditated upon."

"There is nothing else worthwhile thinking, nothing else worthwhile possessing, because nothing worthwhile exists, other than This Atman."

"So, what is it that you are asking for? You are not asking for any object or thing; you are asking for a condition of completeness in your being."

Explaining the concept of love or desire in this way, Yajnavalkya says; "Everything shall leave you if you regard anything as other than, external to you. Anything that is outside you cannot belong to you and cannot satisfy you, and it will leave you. So, it shall bring you sorrow. It is a fact which is eternally true."

"So, Maitreyi," says Yajnavalkya, "It is the supreme self that appears as all these desirable things. The Param Atman, Brahm is the one Reality that masquerades in various forms and names, but this point is not understood."

"Thus, one cannot understand the nature of any object in this world unless one knows the supreme self from where it has come. One may finally realise that everything is connected to everything else in such a way that nothing can be known unless everything is known. So, it is not possible to have complete knowledge of any finite object unless the Infinite itself is known. "

"We can know all things, effects if we can locate their origin, or cause. However, it is not easy to trace the final cause of things, although we may be able to perceive the immediate cause of any phenomenon, as we are limited by the capacity of the mind and the sense-organs."

"Whatever the mind can think and the senses can cognise or perceive – these only are the realities to us as human beings. Because of this limitation, even the minutest investigation into the nature of the cause cannot be regarded as ultimate in space and time."

"But, if it could be possible in some mysterious manner, if the ultimate cause could be discovered, then we would be at once in the presence of a flash of illumination wherein everything is presented before the mind's eyes instantaneously, at one stroke, as it were."

Yajnavalkya tells Maitreyi that when it happens, there would be no bondage. There would be no feeling, hearing, touching, smelling, no consciousness at all.

So bluntly says Yajnavalkya, without commenting on the meaning of this statement, "After dissolution, there is no awareness."

This is what is meant by this pithy statement "Maitreyi, this I tell you. Try to understand it."

सा होवाच मैत्रेय्यत्रैव मा भगवानमूमुहद् न प्रेत्य सञ्ज्ञाऽस्तीति ।
स होवाच न वा अरेऽहं मोहं ब्रवीम्यलं वा अर इदं विज्ञानाय ॥ १३॥

Maitryi is surprised by this blunt statement. She was herself a great philosopher. She asks, "How is it? You are saying that it is an ocean of wisdom, a mass of knowledge, substantiality of everything that is consciousness, and now you say there is no consciousness! When there is an absorption of consciousness into itself and freedom from its entanglement with the elements, you say it knows nothing. How is it possible that it knows nothing, while It is All-knowledge?"

"You do not understand what I say," explained Yajnavalkya to Maitryi. " Our concept of knowledge is not real knowledge. It is the animalistic perception that we usually call knowledge."

यत्र हि द्वैतमिव भवति तदितर इतरं जिघ्रति तदितर इतरं
पश्यति तदितर इतरꣳ शृणोति तदितर इतरमभिवदति
तदितर इतरं मनुते तदितर इतरं विजानाति ।
यत्र वा अस्य सर्वमात्मैवाभूत् तत्केन कं जिघ्रेत्
तत्केन कं पश्येत् तत्केन कꣳ शृणुयात् तत्केन
कमभिवदेत् तत्केन कं मन्वीत तत्केन कं विजानीयात् ।
येनेदꣳ सर्वं विजानाति तं केन विजानीयाद्
विज्ञातारमरे केन विजानीयादिति ॥ १४॥
इति चतुर्थं ब्राह्मणम् ॥

"Where there is a duality between knowledge and an object of knowledge, well, naturally it can be known. Where there is something other than the eye, the eye can see. Where the thought is different from the object that is thought, it is possible to think. Where the object is different from understanding, it is possible to understand that object."

" If a condition can be conceived of where the object of knowledge has melted into the knowledge itself, what could be the knowledge which one can be endowed with? Here the object of the knowledge has become knowledge itself, so there is then no such thing as knowing 'anything', and therefore it is, O Maitryi, that I said no such thing as knowing exists there and it does not know anything."

"There is no such thing as knowing of Knower. Knowing of objects only is there before liberation, or understanding of true self. With liberation, that object has become one with the Knower. The Knower alone is; there is no such thing then as 'knowing'."

*This Vidya is very famous by the name of Maitreyi. T*he pursuit of self-knowledge is considered important in the *Sruti* because the Maitreyi dialogue is repeated in chapter 4.5 as a "logical finale" to the discussion of Brahman in the Upanishad.

The Maitreyi Brahm Vidya is considered one of the most important pearls of wisdom of the Upanishads, and the base of Advait.

Next, we narrate Goddesses described in Vedas.

CHAPTER 7 USHA AND RATRI

Story 1 Usha in Vedas

Usha is the goddess of dawn in Rig Veda. She reveals herself in the daily coming of light to the world. She is celebrated in several hymns for her beauty and vitality. She dispels the darkness and heralds the arrival of the sun.

Usha is seen as a young maiden, drawn in a hundred horses' chariot. She is often invoked for her blessings, representing hope, renewal, and the beginning of a new day.

In a more general aspect, she is the source of all the cosmic forms of consciousness from the physical upwards. The seven rays, *sapta gavah*, are her forms and there are seven names and seven forms or power of this supreme Light, of this supreme Consciousness.

She is also sometimes called Aditi. And in fact, we do find her so described in I.113.19, *mata devanam aditer anıkam*, "Mother of the gods, form (or, power) of Aditi."

Usha is sometimes described as *ritavarı*, showing the True rules, sometimes as *sunritavarı*. She comes uttering the beautiful true rules, Rits.

As she has been described as the leader of the radiant herds and the leader of the days, so she is described as the luminous leader of happy true system, *bhasvatı netrı sunritanam* (I.92.7).

This close connection in the mind of the Vedic Rishis between the idea of light, of the rays, and the idea of the true system, is even more unmistakable in another Rik,

gomati asvavati vibhavari . . . sunritavati, "(I.92.14)
"Dawn with thy shining radiance, with thy swiftness, widely luminous, full of happy truths."
The epithets *gomati* and *asvavati* applied to her are symbolical and mean not "cowful' and 'horsed", but radiant with illuminations of knowledge and accompanied by the swiftness of force.
Usha is *prachetah*, she who that provides this perceptive knowledge. Mother of the radiances, she has created this perceptive vision of the mind;
gavam janitri akrita pra ketum (I.124.5).
She is herself that vision, "Now perceptive vision has broken out into its wide dawn where nought was before."

Story 2 Ratri
Ratri is the goddess of night and is invoked for her protective qualities. She represents the tranquility of night and is often seen as a motherly figure who provides shelter and safety during the darkness.
Let us describe some of her benign qualities. Usually, Ratri is said to be sister of Usha. Together they are called powerful mothers (1.142.7) and strengthener of vital powers (5.5.6).
Together they are also called weavers of time with their alternating, cyclical, and endless appearances, representing stable, rhythmic patterns of the eternal cosmic Rit in which light and dark follow each other. In this way, they illustrate the coherence of the created order, with ordered alteration of vigor and rest, light and dark, and regular flow of time.
Ratri is called glorious and immortal and is praised for providing light in the darkness, being bedecked with countless stars and the Moon. She is praised for bestowing life-sustaining dew and with Usha is said to provide and strengthen vital powers. She is prayed to protect from dangers like wolves, thieves, other creatures.

Ratri is also referred in negative terms, being inimical to

people. She is called barren (1.122.2) and gloomy (10.172.4) in comparison with her sister Usha. She is associated with several dangerous creatures. So, she is chased away by Agni (10.3.1) and also by Usha (1.92.11).

Story 3: How Usha clears negativity of Ratri

In accordance with the ways of Rits, Usha wakes all living things, but does not disturb the person who sleeps in death.

As the recurring dawn, Usha is not only celebrated for bringing light from darkness, she is also petitioned to grant long life, being the constant reminder of peoples' limited time on earth.

The Dawn is also the inner dawn which brings to man all the varied fullness of his widest being, force, consciousness, joy. The Night is clearly the image of an inner darkness; by the coming of the Dawn the Truths are won out of the Nights.

Usha is radiant with its illuminations, it is accompanied by all possible powers and energies, it gives man the full force of vitality so that he can enjoy the infinite delight of that vaster existence.

This is the rising of the Sun which was lost in the obscurity— the familiar figure of the lost sun recovered by the Gods and the Angiras Rishis—the sun of Truth, and it now shoots out its tongue of fire towards the golden Light: —for *hiranya*, golden is the concrete symbol of the higher light, the gold of the Truth, and it is this treasure not golden coin for which the Vedic Rishis pray to the Gods.

The Night of the Veda is the obscured consciousness of the mortal being in which the Truth is hidden in the cave of the hill; that the recovery of the lost sun lying in this darkness of Night is the recovery of the sun of Truth out of the darkened subconscient condition.

CHAPTER 8 PRITHVI AND ADITI

Story 1 Prithvi and Dyau

Prithvi, the Earth Goddess, is invoked in the Rigveda as a nurturing and sustaining force. She represents fertility, abundance, and the physical world. Hymns dedicated to Prithvi celebrate her role in providing sustenance and protection to all living beings.

In Rig Veda, she is always coupled with Dyaus, the male deity associated with the sky. Interdependence is clear from the regular use of the pair as dyava-prithvi.

Together they are said to be universal parents, who created and nurture the world. Together, they kiss the center of world. (1.185.5)

Dyaus fertilizes the earth with rain. Prithvi is praised for her productive and supportive nature. She is firm, broad and wide. She upholds and supports all things (1.18.5).

Prithvi with Dyaus is petitioned for wealth, reaches and power. Also to protect people from danger and sin. A dead man is asked to go to the lap of his mother, earth. Prithvi is asked not to press down too heavily upon the dead person but to cover gently as a mother covers her child with her skirt (10.18. 10-12)

There is a very extended prayer to Prithvi in Atharva Veda (12.1). It is famous as Prithvi-Sukta. Unlike in Rig Veda, it praises the Earth independently without linking with Dyaus.

Repeatedly emphasizing on the fertility of Prithvi, the hymn states that it is the source of all plants, all crops and nourisher of

all creatures. She is patient and firm (12.1.29).
She supports and nurses all his children, both wicked and good, the demons and the gods. Prithvi manifests herself in the scent, or qualities of women and men, to be luck and light in men, and the splendid energy and beauty of maids (12.1.25). She provides sustenance to all those who move upon her broad, firm expanse. Later on, in Puranas, Prithvi is present first in story of Varaha Avatara, when Shri Hari takes the incarnation of a boar to bring up the Prithvi from the depth of Rasatala, and kills the demon Hiranyaksha. The story is narrated in the first part of this series of books.

Again, Prithvi goes to Indra, Brahma, and Vishnu in the story of Krishna Avatar. She is crying because of the burden of Asuras living as Kings and other warriors, and is also afraid of ensuing Kali Yuga. The story is narrated in the second part of the series of books.

The condition of Prithvi after attack of Kali Yuga, as a cow, is narrated in the story of Parikshit, in the first part of this series of books on "Stories from Puranas."

Story 2 Diti and Aditi

Goddess Aditi is mentioned more than eighty times in Rig Veda, usually along with other Gods and Goddesses. It is difficult to understand her because she cannot be linked with any natural phenomena like Usha or Prithvi.

She is often considered the mother of the gods (Devas) and is associated with infinite goodness and following the Ritas, or true cosmic order. She is revered as a nurturing figure and is connected with the idea of freedom and protection.

Aditi is sometimes referred to as the goddess of the dawn and is linked to the concept of the primordial source from which all beings emerge.

Diti is the mother of the Daityas, a group of divine beings often associated with the asuras (demons). While not as prominently worshipped as Aditi, she is mentioned in the context of the cosmic order and the struggles between gods and demons.

Normally, two words are considered opposite to each other. People explain Aditi as A-Diti, privative of Diti. 'Da' root is for binding, and so Diti represents tied up. Aditi is unbound, and so represents infinite qualities. the two words derive from entirely different roots, *ad* and *di*.

Rig Veda says; from Aditi, the Unborn *Para Shakti* was born *Daksha*, the infinitely Able One, the Creator, and again from *Daksha* the *Aditi*, the A*dishakti* was born *(Rig Veda: 10-72-4)*.

Aditi is the mother of seven streams of knowledge and nobility. The immortals Devas took birth from Aditi (Rig Veda: 10-72-5). She is the ultimate creator, and She is the creation.

Aditi, the mother of the Gods, is described both as the Cow, providing knowledge, divine light and nurturing all. She is so known as the general Mother. She is the Supreme Light and all radiances proceed from her.

Psychologically, Aditi is the supreme or infinite Consciousness, mother of the gods, in opposition to Danu or Diti, the divided consciousness, mother of Vritra and the other Danava—enemies of the gods and of man in his progress.

Aditi is pre-eminently the mother of Adityas, a group of seven or eight gods which includes Mitra, Varuna, Aryaman, Bhaga, Daksha, and Ansha (2.27.1). As a mother, Aditi is prayed to guard (1.106.7: 8.18.6). She is also prayed to provide wealth, safety, and abundance (1.94.15). As a cow, she provides nourishment. As a cosmic cow, her milk is identified with the redemptive, invigorating drink Soma (1.153.3).

Aditi is the guardian of Ritas, and status of infinite true order. Adityas are her children and they support the creatures to become Ritavan, or follower of true rules, systems.

In Brahmanas, Aditi is considered as widely expanded and mother of all, and so identified with Prithvi.

CHAPTER 9
SARASVATI IN VEDAS

Story 1 Sarasvati – a river and Goddess of learning

The word "Sarasvati" is derived from the root sru, gatau (सृ, गतौ) or to move. Deriving from this root, one has saras (सरस्), which gives the word Sarasvati.

Saro or saras means knowledge, or transcendental science.

सरो नाम विज्ञानं विद्यतेमस्या सा सरस्वती।

विज्ञानं नाम विविधं यज् ज्ञानं तत् विज्ञानम्— the one in whom such knowledge is sustained is Sarasvati.

Devaraja Yajvan, the commentator on Yaska's Nirukta, derives the word as, सरः प्रसरणमस्यास्तीति, "sarah prasaranamasyastitt'" i.e. Sarasvati is one whose expanse is this entire creation.

Saraswati is mentioned in the Rigveda as a goddess associated with knowledge, wisdom, and the arts. She is linked to the river that bears her name and is often regarded as a source of inspiration for poets and scholars.

According to Aurobindo, Sarasvati means "she of the Stream, the flowing movement", and is therefore, a natural name both for a river and for the goddess of inspiration.

Saraswati is the first of Goddesses eulogized in Rigveda in triplet of Richas 1.3. 10-12.

She is described both as a mighty river, and a Goddess, first as a purifying presence in 1.3.10.

पावका नः सरस्वती वाजेभिर्वाजिनीवती।

यज्ञं वष्टु धियावसुः॥ 1.3 (10)

Next Richa states,

चोदयित्री सुनृताना चेतन्ती सुमतीनाम् ।
यज्ञ दधे सरस्वती ॥ 1.3 (11)

Sarasvati, the inspirer of those who excel in following the Rita, the instructress of the right-minded, may accept and support our great pious work, Yagya.

महो अर्णः सरस्वती प्रचेतयति केतुना ।
धियो बिश्वा विराजति॥ 1.3 (12)

Sarasvati makes manifest by her acts a mighty river and (in her own form) enlightens all intelligence. She incites all pious and gracious thoughts.

These Richas provide a link between the individual minds, and a link between the infinitesimal individual mind and the Super-Mind. Also, a link between the Goddess of intellect and a river of mighty water flow.

As a river, Sarasvati has been called mighty and powerful. Her waves are said to break down mountains, and when full, it roars (6.61.2, 8) She is said to surpass all rivers in largeness, to be ever active, and the greatest.

She is inexhaustible, sourced from the celestial ocean (7.95.1-2; 5.43.11).

She is clearly no mere river, but a heavenly stream that blesses the earth, and the three Lokas (6.61.11-12). She is praised for making the earth fertile. She is also eulogized for wealth, for vitality, for children. She is called bountiful, and best of mothers. (2.41.16)

Her nature is ascetic. She is the bestower of the fruits of the ascetism of the ascetics. She is the Siddhi and Vidyas of all. She grants always success to all.

Were She not here, the whole host of Brahmins would always remain speechless like the dead cluster of persons. What is recited in the Vedas as the Third Devi is the Holy Word.

Saraswati is the Presiding Deity of knowledge, speech, intelligence, and learning. She is all the learning of this endless Universe and She resides as Medha (intelligence) in the hearts of all the human beings. She is the power in composing poetry.

She is the memory and She is the great wit, light, splendor and inventive genius. She gives the power to understand the real meaning of the various difficult Siddhanta works.

She makes us understand the difficult passages and She is the remover of all doubts and difficulties. She blesses when we write books, when we argue and judge, when we sing songs of music. She is the time or meter in music; She holds balance and union in vocal and instrumental music. She is the Goddess of speech. She is the Presiding Deity in the knowledge of various subjects; in argumentations and disputations.

In fact, all the beings earn their livelihood by taking recourse to Her. She is peaceful and holds in Her hands Vina (lute) and books. Her nature is purely Sattvic (Shuddha Sattva), modest and very loving to Shri Hari. Her color is white like ice-clad mountains, like that of the white sandal, like that of the Kunda flower, like that of the Moon, or white lotus.

Story 2: Sarasvati as a manifestation of Ishwar

Sarasvati, without the least doubt is the Divine Speech (Ait. Br. II. 24; III. 1, 2). She is plainly and clearly, the Goddess of Word, if we speak in terms of symbolism. Ishwar has manifested Himself in His creation, and in His word as knowledge personified.

We have a very significant verse in which the Supreme Lord is represented as Sarasvati:

सरस्वतीं देवयन्तो हवन्ते सरस्वतीमध्वरे तायमाने |
सरस्वतीं सुकृतो अह्वयन्त सरस्वती दाशुषे वार्य दात् || (Rv.X.17.7)

Men aspiring for transcendental knowledge invoke the Lord Sarasvati. When one aspires to undertake sacred works for the good of all (adhvara), they also invoke Sarasvati. This Sarasvati blesses all of them who dedicate themselves for noble ends.

The word Sarasvati occurs in three contexts particularly: (1) her invocation alone, (ii) her invocation along with the terms as Ila, Mahi and Bharati, and (iii) her invocation along with seven Sindhu, understood as the names of several rivers in Northern India

Story 3 Ila, Sarasvati, Bharati (or Mahi)

Normally Mahi and Bharati are consider identical.

For we have a reference to "tisro devir" (the three enlightened divine powers):

इळा सरस्वती मही तिस्रो देवीर्मयोभुवः।
बर्हिः सीदन्त्वस्त्रिधः॥ (Rv. 1. 13.9)

"May lla, Sarasvati, and Mahi, three goddesses, divine powers of examining properties, of flowing intelligence, and of cosmic true rules, who give blissfulness to all, enlighten all houses, and every Yagya seats.

The same idea occurs in another verse of the Rigveda:

आ देवीबं नो यज्ञ भारती तूयमंत्विख मनुष्यवदिह चेतगन्ती।
हि रेदं स्योनं सरस्वती स्वपसः सदन्त्॥ (Rv. X. 110.8)

May Bharati come speeding to our Yagya and hither awakening our human consciousness (or perception), and Sarasvati, —three goddesses sit on this blissful seat, doing well the work.

Considering the various passages of the Vedic Texts, Aurobindo comes to the conclusion that Sarasvati word, the inspiration that comes from the Rita, the Truth-Consciousness, of knowledge, of Light in the Veda is a symbol of spiritual illumination.

Surya is the lord of supreme sight, the Vast Light; brhat jyotih (बृहत् ज्योतिः) or the True-Light, ritam jyotih (ऋतं ज्योतिः).

Shall we not associate a sort of parallelism between Satyam, Ritam and Brihat on the one hand, Sarasvati, Ila and largeness, mahi on the other?

Mahi is the luminous vastness of Truth; she represents the Brihat, of the super-conscient in us. She is, therefore, for 'containing in itself the true way, Ritam.'

Ritam Brihat (ऋतं बृहत) is the same as Maho Arnaha (महो अर्णः) or the Cosmic Mind or Cosmic Intelligence of the Vedic Texts.

There is a good deal of sense when Aurobindo (Vol. X. p. 91) says, that as Sarasvati represents the true rule or process— revelation, Sruti, (श्रुति) which gives the inspired word, so Ila represents Dristi (दृष्टि) or truth-vision.

Thus, Dristi and Sruti are the two powers of the seer of the truth (Kavi or Risi), which provides a close relation between Ila and Sarasvati.

In the first Richa itself, अग्नि-ईडे, Ida is meaning observation of properties of Agni, and not necessarily prayer of Agni.

Then, Bharati or mahi is the largeness of truth-consciousness, Which, dawning on man's limited mind brings with it the two sisters. This is one way of explaining the triad.

This planes also: Satyam Ritam Brhat, triad has also to be worked out on this triad of Truth-observation, Ida - Dristi, insight, Sarasvati Sruti, and Mahi (Bharati), Large, National Character, language, or Culture.

Story 4 Sarasvati as one of the Seven rivers (Sapta sindhus).

We observe Sarasvati being presented as one of the seven rivers. Some take these as seven rivers of Punjab, out of which Sarasvati is one. Question arises as to what is the idea of seven rivers always associated together (sapta-sindhavah, सप्तसिन्धवः) in the minds of the sages and all of them released together.

How the general idea of the river of inspiration come to be associated with a particular earthly stream out of seven, by its surroundings, natural and legendary, which might seem more fitfully associated with the idea of sacred inspiration than any other.

It seems impossible to suppose that one river only in all this sevenfold outflowing acquired a psychological significance while the rest were associated only with the annual coming of the rains. (Aurobindo, Vol. X. p. 88)

The Vedic literature is abundantly rich in referring to heptads or groups of seven, and we understand their scientific relevance and meaning now. There are rays of seven colors, signifying seven horses of the Sun, the seven delights, Sapta ratnani (सप्त रत्नानि), and seven tongues or flames of fire, Sapta arcisali (सप्ताचिष:), or Sapta jvalah (सप्त ज्वाला:).

Similarly, we have Sapta sindhavah (सप्त सिन्धवः), or seven mothers, Sapta matarah, seven notes of sound, Sapta dhenavah (सप्त धेनवः), and of course the Seven seers (Great Bears), Sapta risayah.

And in I.72.8, speaking of them in a phrase which is applied to the rivers in other hymns, Ishwar says,

"The seven mighty ones of heaven, placing aright the thought, knowing the Truth, discerned in knowledge the doors of felicity; Sarama found the fastness, the wideness of the luminous cows; thereby the human creature enjoys the bliss,"

svadhyo diva a sapta yahvi, rayo duro vi ritajna⁻ ajanan; vidad gavyam˙

sarama⁻ dridham u⁻ rvam˙ , yena⁻ nu kam˙ manusı⁻ bhojate vit..

These are evidently the rivers of Heaven, the streams of the Truth, goddesses like Saraswati, who possess the Truth in knowledge and open by it the doors of the beatitude to the human creature.

It is now perfectly clear that the achievement of the Angiras is the conquest of the Truth and the Immortality, that Swar called also the great heaven, B*rihat dyauh* , is the plane of the Truth above the ordinary heaven and earth which can be no other than the ordinary mental and physical being.

That the path of the great heaven, the path of the Truth created by the Angirases and followed by the hound Sarama is the path to the Immortality, *amritatvaya guatum.*

Thus, the vision (*ketu*) of the Dawn, the Day won by the Angiras, is the vision proper to the Truth-consciousness; that the luminous rays of the Sun and Dawn wrested from the Panis, powers preventing the true conscience, are the illuminations of this truth-consciousness which help to form the thought of the Truth, *ritasya dhitih.*

The seven rivers downflowing earthward including Sarasvati must be the out-streaming action of the sevenfold principle of our being as it is formulated in the Truth of the divine or immortal existence, or Rits.

Vritra must be the power that obstructs and prevents the free movement of the illumined rivers of the Truth, obstructs the impulsion of the Truth in us, *Ritasya presa*, the luminous impulsion, J*yotismatım isam*, which carries us beyond the Night to the immortality.

And the gods, the sons of Aditi, must be on the contrary the luminous divine powers, born of the infinite consciousness Aditi, whose formation and activity in our human and mortal being are necessary for our growth into the godhead, into the being of the divine qualities (*devatvam*) which is the Immortality.

This immortality is described as a beatitude, a state of infinite spiritual wealth and plenitude, *ratna, rayi, vaja, radhas*, etc., and the opening doors of our divine home are the doors of the felicity, *rayo durah.*, the divine doors which swing wide open to those who increase the True rules or systems (*ritavridhah*).

These Rits are discovered for us by Saraswati and her sisters, by the seven Rivers, by Sarama; to them and to the wide pasture (*kshetra*) in the unobstructed and equal infinities of the vast Truth Brihaspati and Indra lead upward the shining Herds.

Here is the explanation of Sarasvati always expressed as one of the seven rivers.

CHAPTER 10 VAK DEVI

Story 1 Vak Devi

We discuss the Vak Devi just after Saraswati since in other scriptures, Vak Devi is not considered different from Saraswati. However, she also represents the Param Shakti.

The Goddess Vac, whose name means speech, reveals herself through speech and is typically characterized by various attributes and uses of speech. She inspires the rishis. She is truth. She is the power of hearing, and of seeing, understanding and expressing through words the true nature of things, and the Rita.

Reflecting her role as the bestower of vision, Vac is called the queen of all divine powers (8.89). She is also known as bestower of vital powers (3.53.15).

She is described as a courtly, elegant woman, bright and adorned with gold (1.167.3). Like Sarasvati, she is a benign, bounteous Goddess. She is a nourishing deity, and often been invoked as a heavenly cow (4.1.16; 4.8.89).

Bearing her mark of intelligible, familiar speech, one friend may recognize and commune with another. Without her, the divine rituals would not have been possible to be performed.

Vac plays a significant role in Vedic literature from a theoretical point of view. Her role in Brahmanas is suggestive of the nature of Shakti in later Scriptures.

Next, we discuss a great Rishika of Rig Veda, to whom the famous Vak Shukta is attributed to.

Story 2: The great Rishika Vagambhrini

Vagambhrini is one of the great female poet-seer mentioned in Rig Veda. She was the daughter of Rishi Ambhrina and is so known as Rishika Vagambhrini.

Her name is combined with two words Vak (meaning speech or Vaagdevi) and that of her father, Rishi Ambhrina. She is regarded as the avatar of goddess Vak or Saraswati, the Adi Shakti.

After attaining the *samadhi*, or highest consciousness through meditation in a *Rishi*-like-state when one has a glimpse of Knowledge of the Rits governing self and cosmos, she realized *"Aham Brahmasmi"* which means "I am the Brahman" or "I am the Absolute".

She finds her existence integral to that of the Goddess of speech or Vaagdevi. Her hymns appear in Rig Veda, Mandala 10, Sukta 125 as Vak Sukta.

It is also known as Aatma Sukta – the song of the Self or Devi Sukta – the song of Devi. The eight verses in this Sukta explain the realization of the Absolute as the Self.

The Advait, or oneness of the individual self with the Shakti or Brahm is described in the Vak Shukta, and that too, in a feminine perspective.

Vak Sukta hymns are sacred with spiritual knowledge and ritual chants. She is treated as Jagat Janani – the mother of the universe as the creator, and is called *Prakriti*, Mother Nature. She is a feminine manifested form of the Absolute; or Brahm. In fact, all the manifestation is feminine, it is *prakriti* (nature).

The *Devi* makes it possible for rishis – the learned seers and sages – to hear, grasp, and reveal the truths of pure existence, to devise, and create the hymns and rituals that express the knowledge of their visions in a Rishi-like-state.

She bestows vision on the seers. She gives wisdom to the wise. She is the energy principle of this universe. She is the center of the creation of all wisdom. In *Vak Sukta* she says (here the first and last verses of the *Sukta* are given below);

ॐ अहं रुद्रेभिर्वसुभिश्चराम्यहमादित्यैरुत विश्वदेवैः ।
अहं मित्रावरुणोभा बिभर्म्यहमिन्द्राग्नी अहमश्विनोभा ॥ १॥

Aham rudrebhir vasubhis charāamyaham ādityair uta visvadevaihû

Aham mitra varunobhā bibharmyaham indrāgni aham asvinobhā. (Atmasukta: 1)

I move with the Rudras and also with the Vasus, I walk with the Adityas and the Vishwa devas. I hold both Mitra and Varuna, and also Indra and Agni, and the twin Ashvini Kumaras.

Here Vaagdevi teaches that the entire world appears in the Self only. The substratum of all these names and forms, from Rudras to Ashvini Kumaras, is nothing but the Self.

अहमेव वात इव प्र वाम्यारभमाणा भुवनानि विश्वा ।
परो दिवा पर एना पृथिव्यैतावती महिना सं बभूव ॥ ८॥

Ahameva vāta iva pra vāmi arabhamānā bhuvanāni vishvā;

Paro divā para enā prithivi etāvatī mahinā sam babhûva. (Ātmasûkta: 2)

I blow as the mighty wind on my own without being directed by anyone else, I as the cause, hold together all these worlds. I am beyond the heavens and above the earth, such am I in my might and fame.

This means she says; "I am the cause, power, and strength of this world. I am the knowledge; I am the one who gives food, the wind which the beings breathe, and so on. I am beyond all the manifestations. Though I am everything still I am untouched, unattached. I am the Absolute Consciousness. I move with my own glory".

The Devi Sukta (10.125) is another striking example of a Samhita mantra depicting Advaita experience.

She (the rishi) had known or realized as her own Self the supreme Brahman, that which must be realized. Here, Brahma is in feminine form

CHAPTER 11 GAYATRI AS PER VEDA

Story 1: Triplet in chapter three of Rig Veda

The earliest presence of the Gayatri Mantra is in the Rig Veda, where it is part of a hymn dedicated to several gods at the end of the third book (III 62). It is attributed to Vishvamitra Gathina

It is composed in triplets (Trichas), groups of three Richas or "verses describing Rit" that are frequently set in the gayatri meter. Rig Veda III 62 comprises six Trichas (i.e., eighteen verses).

It is very famous and the best-known verse of Rig Veda. The Gayatri Mantra is the first verse of the fourth triplet of the tripartite hymn. This triplet (RV III 62.10–12) is here given as a whole:

तत्सवितुर्वरेण्यं भर्गो देवस्य धीमहि।

धियो यो नः प्रचोदयात्॥

tát savitúr váreṇiyaṃ
 bhárgo devásya dhīmahi
 dhíyo yó naḥ pracodáyāt /10/

May we obtain that desirable splendour of the god Impeller, who shall spur on our thoughts! /10/

देवस्य सवितुर्वयं वाजयन्तः पुरन्ध्या।

भगस्य रातिमीमहे॥

devásya savitúr vayáṃ vājayántaḥ púraṃdhiyā
 bhágasya rātím īmahe /11/

Competing for the generosity of the god Impeller, we ask for the gift, our portion of the Apportioned fortune. /11/

देवं नरः सवितारं विप्रा यज्ञैः सुवृक्तिभिः ।
नमस्यन्ति धियेषिताः ॥

devám náraḥ savitāraṃ víprā yajñáiḥ suvṛktíbhiḥ /
namasyánti dhiyéṣitāḥ /12/
To the god Impeller do the men, as inspired ones, give reverence
with Yagya and well written verses, when driven by thoughts
inspired by Him. /12/

Story 2: Meaning of each letter
tát - "that", something well-known to all of us
savitúr- "existing in" Savita, or the Impeller, or Initiator, or
Instigator"; Sanskrit also "of the Sun" derived from the root sū
várenyam- "desirable, excellent, respectable
bhárgo - "splendour, effulgence, radiance"
devásya- of the god , of the divine Brahma
"dhīmahi- may we / would we / we wish to" + "obtain/attain/
receive/ make our own"
"we have obtained", first person plural in the middle voice of the
aorist optative or injunctive of dhā;
Alternative meaning "(may) we contemplate/visualize" Sanskrit
speakers also interpreted it as a "Vedic" first person plural of the
present indicative or optative of 'dhī' "thoughts, inspirations"
dhíyo - dhíyas, accusative plural of the feminine noun dhī, root-
noun derived from dhī "thoughts, inspirations"
yó - "who" sandhi form of yáḥ,
 naḥ "our" asmākam,
prachodáyāt - "shall/will" + "spur on /inspire/stimulate" the
causative of prá+chud;

Story 3: Savita
In the Vedic language, Savita is an agent noun derived from
the root sū (or secondary su) "to impel," which has to be
distinguished from the homophone sū "to give birth to."
Savita thus literally means "impeller, initiator, arouser
instigator" or "stimulator."
Thus, Savita impels gods, humans and animals to action. He

causes the change of day and night as well as the seasons and is also responsible for the movement of rivers and the wind. he continued to be known for his function as the divine impeller even in the post-Vedic period.

While later, the Sun came to be seen as his only manifestation, and the word Savita was frequently used as a synonym of Surya, he remained a distinct (Vedic) God, and continued to function as a god of fecundity and procreation– an "impeller of new life."

Story 4: Bharga

But what is Bharga? And why would one want to obtain it?

bhrāj (from root 'bherHg̊) suggests that it may denote a kind of light that evokes the impression of (1) an unsteady flicker as in the case of flames, or (2) movement and effulgence as in the case of the sun. In the Rig Veda, the term appears only three times; two times connected with Agni, the god of fire.

In view of Savita's association with the early morning and evening, it is conceivable that 'Bharga' in the Gayatri Mantra indeed denotes some kind of physical light, such as, perhaps, the gentle gleam of the sky before sunrise and after sunset.

Now, the visions or inspiration of the Vedic poets are often said to be transmitted early in the morning as sung in Riks associated with Usha. Being, in a very general sense, a prayer for inspiration, it might even have been composed and used just at that time.

Now if 'yo' is for this bharga, then bhárgas becomes the agent of pracodáyāt, "shall inspire" or "set in motion." "Savitu" is indicative of that available in Savita. Thus, this Bharga is the effulgence, the gentle gleam of Savita, practically known as Sun.

In several Brahmanas, bhargas (sometimes in the form bhárga) is equated with Virya, or "heroic power" or "vigor," which the personified Waters take from Varuna when he is consecrated.

It is also frequently associated or mentioned alongside várchas "luster," yáśas "fame," ójas "vigor," bála "strength," máhas "greatness," srī "splendor," yajñasya yad yaśas that "which is the fame of the sacrifice," yajñásya yát páyas that "which is the essence of the sacrifice,"bhaga "portion" and stoma "praise."

This makes it likely that in the Rig Veda, too, the word does not necessarily denote the inspiring "gleam" of Savita in the early morning, but a somewhat less sublime "splendor" or "glory."

Story 5: Savitri The "Mother of the Vedas"

It is this "Effulgence" of the Savita, who is at the centre of the mantra and is worthy of visualization or contemplation.

In feminine form the Bharga, or effulgence of the supreme God is called Savitri.

Savitri is Ved Mata, because for the composers of the Rig Veda, light, intuition, inspiration and the act of composing hymns were integrally related.

First, Vedic poets thought that hymns appealing to the gods should be inspired by something already existent, rather than being created "out of nothing." They considered their ideas and inspirations to be something that must be received, not produced.

Second, they felt inspiration and insight to be a kind of sight or vision.

So, each of the Richas of Rig veda is produced from the Bharga, or effulgence of Ishvara, which is known as Savitri.

Savitri mantra is metered in Gayatri Chhand, and so also called Gayatri.

This is why Gayatri is called Ved Mata.

Story 6: Ved Mata

Ved Mata Is an epithet and alternative name that is used quite frequently for the Gayatri Mantra as well as for its deification.

Among the earliest texts to use the expression is the Mahabharat, where it occurs (at least) five times, mostly in the Shanti Parva as well as in the appendices.

The Shanti Parva in particular contains a number of passages where the "Mother of the Vedas" comes to the fore. In two of them, she appears to humans in a visible form. The emergence of the mantra goddess was also facilitated by another process, namely the identification of the mantra with a pre-existent goddess.

Savita is the Presiding Deity of the Surya mandala, the solar orb.

The Sun is the central Para Brahma. The Gayatri Mantra, the Presiding Devi, proves the existence of the Bharga of the highest Brahma in the center of the Sun.

Therefore, she is called Savitri. Or Her name is Savitri because all the Vedas have come out of Her.

Next, we narrate a great Brahm Vidya, which explains the way Gayatri recitation leads one to Brahma, and protection.

CHAPTER 12 GAYATRI VIDYA IN UPANISHAD

Story 1 Meaning as per Chhandogya Upanishad

The Gayatri is a Mantra well-known to people.

ॐ भूर्भुवः स्वः
तत्सवितुर्वरेण्यं
भर्गो देवस्य धीमहि।
धियो यो नः प्रचोदयात्॥

Gayantam trayati gayatri: One who protects that devotee who by singing, chanting, or reciting, resorts to this Mantra is Gayatri. As per Chhandogya Upanishad

गायत्री वा ईदꣳ सर्वं भूतं यदिदं किं च वाग्वै गायत्री
वाग्वा इदꣳ सर्वं भूतं गायति च त्रायते च ॥ ३.१२.१॥

The gayatri is everything, whatever here exists. Speech is verily the Gayatri, for speech sings forth (gaya—ti) and protects (traya—te) everything, whatever here exists.

सैषा चतुष्पदा षड्विधा गायत्री तदेतदृचाभ्यनूक्तम् ॥ ३.१२.५॥

That Gayatri has four feet and is sixfold. The same is also declared by a Rik—verse.

This is a Mantra with twenty-four letters, three feet and three quarters. The fourth foot is a mystical one about which the Upanishad will be mentioning something very special towards the end.

Story 2: Meditation as per Brihadaranyaka Upanishad

Now, how do we contemplate the feet of Gayatri? It is a chant of the Veda.

Methods of meditation on the correspondence between the

letters of the different feet of Gayatri with certain other visible phenomena in life are prescribed in Brihadaranyaka Upanishad, as follows:

भूमिरन्तरिक्षं द्यौरित्यष्टावक्षराण्यष्टाक्षरꣳ ह वा एकं
गायत्र्यै पदमेतदु हैवास्या एतत्
स यावदेषु त्रिषु लोकेषु तावद्ध
जयति योऽस्या एतदेवं पदं वेद ॥ V.xiv.1 ॥

bhūmir antarikṣaṁ dyauḥ ity aṣṭāv akṣarāni;
aṣṭākṣaraṁ ha vā ekaṁ
gāyatryai padametadu haivāsyā etat,

Bhumi is earth; Antariksha is atmosphere; Dyau is heaven. These are designated by three words, three epithets or names, and these names are constituted of eight letters. Similar is the case with each foot of the Gayatri Mantra, which is of eight letters.

Story 3 Meditation on first foot

So, a correspondence is established in meditation between the eight letters of the first foot of Gayatri and the earth, atmosphere, and heaven. In this manner, the first foot of Gayatri mantra is made equivalent to the entire visible world.

sa yāvad eṣu triṣu lokeṣu, tāvaddha jayati,
yo'syā etad evaṁ padaṁ veda

These three worlds – the physical, the atmospheric and the celestial – are supposed to be designated again by what is called the Vyahritis. Vyahritis is what precedes the chant of Gayatri. Bhur, Bhuva, and Svah are the three words, meaning Bhumi, Antariksa, and Dyau, which are called Vyahritis. So is the first foot of Gayatri, which represents the three worlds.

So, here a symbolic meditation is prescribed. One who meditates on the first foot of Gayatri, by identifying its letters with the three worlds, attains to the three worlds. He attains to the Supernal status of Mastery over the earth, atmosphere, and celestial realms. Whatever is there in these three worlds, that this person will win.

It is very difficult to conceive or imagine all this while meditating, but they are very effective techniques as prescribed by the sages with full confidence.

They state that mere contemplation on this correspondence between the letters of the first foot of Gayatri and the letters in the three words, Bhumi, Antariksa, Dyau, will cause the meditator to go to the realm where he becomes a master of the three worlds, is indeed miraculous.

Story 4 Meditation on second foot

ऋचो यजूꣳषि सामानीत्यष्टावक्षराण्यष्टाक्षरꣳ ह वा एकं
गायत्रै पदम् ।

एतदु हैवास्या एतत् स यावतीयं त्रयी विद्या तावद्ध
ह जयति योऽस्या एतदेवं पदं वेद ॥ V.xiv.2 ॥

rco yajūmṣi sāmāni, ity aṣṭāv akṣarāṇi;
aṣṭākṣaraṁ ha vā ekaṁ gāyatrai padam.

Richo Yajusi Samani represent all verses in the three Vedas – Rig, Yajur, and Sama. These again have eight letters, and so maybe considered to be in correspondence with the eight letters of the second foot of the Gayatri.

etad u haivāsyā etat. sa yāvadīyaṁ trayī vidyā,
tāvad ha jayati. yo'syā etad evaṁ padaṁ veda.

One who meditates in the similar manner, concentrating his mind on the correspondence between eight letters of the second foot of Gayatri with the three Vedas, becomes a master of the three Vedas, and attains to realms which are accessible to anyone who is a Master of the three Vedas.

Whatever is capable of being achieved through the three Vedas, that one achieves through the meditation on the second foot of the Gayatri Mantra alone, just as one attains to mastery over the three worlds by contemplation merely on the first foot of the Gayatri.

Story 5 Meditation on third foot

प्राणोऽपानो व्यान इत्यष्टावक्षराणि अष्टाक्षरꣳ ह वा एकं गायत्रै
पदमेतदु हैवास्या एतत् स यावदिदं प्राणि तावद्ध जयति योऽस्या
एतदेवं पदं वेद अथास्या एतदेव तुरीयं दर्शतं पदं परोरजा य
एष तपति यद्वै चतुर्थं तत्तुरीयं दर्शतं पदमिति ददृश
इव ह्येष परोरजा इति सर्वमु ह्येवैष रज उपर्युपरि तपत्येवꣳ
हैव श्रिया यशसा तपति योऽस्या एतदेवं पदं वेद ॥ V.xiv.3 ॥

prāṇo'pāno vyānaḥ, ity aṣṭāv akṣarāṇi;

aṣṭākṣaraṁ ha vā ekaṁ gāyatrai padam:
Now the third foot is mentioned. There are the three essential life-energies, Pranas in the system – Prana, Apana and Vyana. The letters are eight here, again. They have to be set in correspondence with the third foot of the Gayatri mantra which is also constituted of eight letters.

etad u haivāsyā etat. sa yāvad idam prāṇi,
    tāvad ha jayati yo'syā
When you meditate on the third pada of Gayatri considering it to contain Prana, Apan and Vyan, a new miracle takes place. You become a Master of all the worlds constituted of living beings, who depend on the Pran.

One lords over all, as it were, among the realms that are living, provided he contemplates on this correspondence between the letters of the third foot of Gayatri with the three energies within the life system – Prana, Apana, Vyana.

Story 6 Meditation on fourth foot

Etad evam padaṁ veda. athāsya etad eva turīyaṁ darśatam padam: parorajā ya eṣa tapati;
yad vai caturthaṁ tat turīyam; darśatam padam iti, dadṛśa iva. hy eṣaḥ; parorajā iti,
Generally, people do not know that there is any such thing as the fourth foot of Gayatri. Nobody chants the fourth foot. It is a mystical hidden Pada. The fourth Pada is beyond all Rajas Gunas, all properties.

It is something like the Amantra aspect of Pranava, the soundless aspect of Om which is spiritual, which is Consciousness in its essentiality.

While the three feet of Gayatri may be said to comprehend everything that is temporal, the fourth foot is non-temporal.

It represents an absolute state. It is a special feature of this mystical aspect of Gayatri's recitation into which very few people are initiated. Generally, initiation is limited to three feet.

The fourth foot is not visible. One cannot understand what this fourth foot is. To us, it is like a fourth dimension without any sense, but it conveys every sense and every meaning from its own point of view.

This fourth foot is something very mystical.

"It is above the dust of the earth. It is superior to all that is manifest as creation. It is not material at all, and therefore it is called Paroraja. It is super-physical."

sarvam u hy evaiṣa raja upari upari tapati.

 evaṁ haiva śriyā, yaśasā tapati,

yo'syā etad evam padaṁ veda.

'The one that shines before us', the Surya, or the sun, is the supreme reality, the great superintending power, the deity behind this fourth foot of Gayatri. He is to be meditated upon through the recitation of the fourth foot.

'The meditation here is on the Purusha in the sun, not merely on the physical orb of the sun.'

This is a spiritual energy that is resplendent in the sun that is the object of meditation here.

The deity, the divinity which is superior to the physical form of the sun, that deity, that Purusha, Hiranmaya Purusha, is the object of meditation during the chant of the fourth foot of Gayatri Mantra.

'Such a person who knows and contemplates in this manner on the inner significance of this fourth foot, is glorified in this world, endowed with all prosperity, becomes renowned in every respect and shines like the sun himself, as it were.

Importance of contemplation on fourth foot

सैषा गायत्र्येतस्मिꣳस्तुरीये दर्शते पदे परोरजसि प्रतिष्ठिता

तद्वै तत्सत्ये प्रतिष्ठितं चक्षुर्वै सत्यं चक्षुर्हि

वै सत्यं तस्माद्यदिदानीं द्वौ विवदमानावेयातामहम् अदर्श

अहमश्रौषमिति य एव एवं ब्रूयादहम् अदर्शमिति तस्मा एव

श्रद्ध्याम । तद्वै तत्सत्यं बले प्रतिष्ठितं प्राणो वै बलं

तत्प्राणे प्रतिष्ठितं तस्मादाहुर्बलꣳ सत्यादोगीय इत्येवं वेषा

गायत्र्यध्यात्मं प्रतिष्ठिता । सा हैषा गयाꣳस्त्रे प्राणा वै

गयास्तत्प्राणाꣳस्त्रे तद्यद्गयाꣳस्त्रे तस्माद् गायत्री नाम ।

स यामेवामूꣳ सावित्रीमन्वाहैषैव सा ।

स यस्मा अन्वाह तस्य प्राणाꣳस्त्रायते ॥ V.xiv.4 ॥

saiṣā gāyatry etasmiṁs turīye darśate pade parorajasi

68

pratiṣṭhitā,

'The entire Gayatri Mantra is really rooted in the fourth foot.'

It is the Prana Sakti, it is the essence, as it were, of the whole Gayatri. It is the ocean into which the river of the Gayatri Mantra enters. It is the ultimate meaning of the Gayatri.

Just as the non-temporal, the meta-empirical, or the spiritual includes within itself all that is temporal and manifest, so is the fourth foot inclusive of all the meaning that is contained in the first three feet.

tad vai tat *satye pratiṣṭhitam.*

Cakṣur vai satyam, cakṣur hi vai satyam:

tasmād yad idānīṁ dvau vivadamānāv

  eyātām aham adarśam,

we need to meditate on the fourth foot of Gayatri as the ultimate truth. It is the truth that is symbolized by the actual perception of values through the eyes which are presided over by the sun, which again is the deity of the fourth foot of the Gayatri Mantra.

aham aśurauṣam iti. ya eva evaṁ brūyāt;

  aham adarśam iti, tasmā eva śraddadhyāma.

tad vai tat satyaṁ bale pratiṣṭhitam; prāṇo vai balam;

tat prāṇe pratiṣṭhitam; tasmād āhuḥ:

balaṁ satyād ogīya iti.

evaṁ veṣā gāyatry adhyātmam. pratiṣṭhitā

sā haisā gāyāṁs tatre; prāṇā vai gayāḥ;

tat prāṇāṁs tatre; tad yad gayāṁs tatre,

  tasmād gāyatrī nāma.

The capacity to visualize things in their truth is coincident with increased energy and power or capacity. So, one is expected to meditate on Sakti, or Bala, or power, or energy, which follows automatically in the wake of this meditation. This capacity leads us to Adhyatmik realisation.

Story 7: Savitri and Gayatri Mantra

This is what provides protection when one chants, sings the Mantra. This is the reason of calling this Mantra Gayatri also.

sa yām evāmūṁ sāvitrīm anvāha,

  eṣaiva sā. sa yasmā anvāha,

tasya prāṇāṁs trāyate.

Sometimes people call the Gayatri Mantra, Savitri Mantra. The Upanishad says both mean one and the same thing. It is Savitri because it relates to Savitri, or the sun. It is Gayatri because it protects whoever chants it. Your Pranas are protected by this Mantra. Therefore, it is called Savitri; therefore, it is also called Gayatri.

ताᳵ हैतामेके सावित्रीमनुष्टुभमन्वाहुर्वागनुष्टुब्
एतद्वाचमनुब्रूम इति ।
न तथा कुर्याद् गायत्रीमेवानुब्रूयाद् ।
यदि ह वा अप्येवंविद्ध्विव
प्रतिगृह्णाति न हैव तद्गायत्र्या एकं चन पदं प्रति ॥ V.xiv.5 ॥

Tām haitām eke sāvritrīm anuṣṭubham anvāhuḥ:

There is another Savitri Mantra chanted in Anustubh metre constituted of thirty-two letters.

Gayatri is a Mantra; and it is a deity. Now, Gayatri metre is of twenty-four letters. But Anustubh is another metre which has thirty-two letters.

vāg anuṣṭup; etad vācam anubrūma iti.

na tathā kuryāt gāyatrīm eva sāvitrīm anubrūyāt.

 yadi ha vā apy evaṁ-vid bahv

The Upanishad says, 'That is not the proper Gayatri. You should not chant this.'

The proper Savitri Mantra is the one which is in the Gayatri Metre, not the Anustubh one.

'There are some people who think that the Anustubh Mantra is the real Savitri one.'

'It is not so,' 'The Savitri Mantra should be chanted in Gayatri Metre only.

Story 8 What is the glory of this Gayatri?

iva pratigrhṇāti, na haivatad gāyatryā ekaṁ cana padam prati.

Even one single foot of Gayatri, when it is recited, meditated properly, will take you to such realms of glory and magnificence, which transcend in magnitude anything that you can receive as a gift in this world.

स य इमाᳵस्त्रींल्लोकान्पूर्णान्प्रतिगृह्णीयात्

सोऽस्या एतत्प्रथमं पदमाप्नुयाद् ।
अथ यावतीयं त्रयी विद्या यस्तावत्प्रतिगृह्णीयात्
सोऽऽस्या एतद्द्वितीयं पदमाप्नुयादथ यावदिदं प्राणि
यस्तावत्प्रतिगृह्णीयात् सोऽस्या एतत्तृतीयं पदमाप्नुयादथास्या
एतदेव तुरीयं दर्शतं पदं परोरजा य एष तपति नैव केन
चनाप्यं कुत उ एतावत्प्रतिगृह्णीयात् ॥ V.xiv.6॥

sa ya imāṁs trīn lokān pūrṇān pratigṛhṇīyāt,
so'syā etat prathamam padam āpnuyāt;'

When you chant with concentration the first Pada, first foot of the Gayatri Mantra, you become endowed with mastery over the three worlds.

atha yāvatīyaṁ trayī vidyā, yas tāvat pratigṛhnīyāt,
so'syā etad dvitīyam padam āpnuyāt;

If you can chant correctly even the second foot merely, you become endowed with all the glory that comes to one by study of the three Vedas.

atha yāvad idam prāṇi, yas tāvat pratigṛhnīyāt,
so'syā etat tṛtīyam padam āpnuyāt,

If you recite the third foot of the Gayatri Mantra, you become capacitated to rule over every living being anywhere.

athāsyā etad eva turīyaṁ darśataṁ padam,
parorajā ya eṣa tapati, naiva kena canāpyam;
kuta u etāvat pratigṛhnīyāt.

If you are to meditate on the fourth foot of Gayatri, what can I tell you? How can I explain to you the glory that will come to you? Nothing of this world can equal that. No gift of the three worlds can equal the glory.

Not the three Vedas, not all beings put together, not mastery over all living beings, nothing mentioned up to this time can equal the glory that comes to one who meditates on this fourth foot of Gayatri.

That glory is inexpressible; it is transcendent; it is superior to everything which is material or visible.

तस्या उपस्थानं गायत्र्यस्येकपदी द्विपदी
त्रिपदी चतुष्पद्यपदसि न हि पद्यसे ।
नमस्ते तुरीयाय दर्शताय पदाय परोरजसेऽसावदो मा प्रापदिति

यं द्विष्यादसावस्मै कामो मा समृद्धीति वा न हैवास्मै स
कामः समृद्ध्यते यस्मा एवमुपतिष्ठतेऽहमदः प्रापमिति वा ॥ V.xiv.7 ॥

tasyā upasthānam: gāyatri,

One should worship or pray to Gayatri by certain methods. One of the methods is a verbal chant, a prayer offered to the great deity of the Gayatri. A particular chant is given here.

asy eka-padī dvi-padī tri-padī chatuṣ-pady
a-pad asi, na hi padyase.

'O Gayatri, the great one! You are one-footed, two-footed, three-footed and you possess the fourth foot also as the case may be. You are everything, but really you have no feet. That is also true. But these feet are only concepts in our mind. You are universal, all-pervading, all-comprehensive being. You never move anywhere.

namas te turīyāya darśatāya padāya parorajase;
asāv ado mā prāpad iti;

"We bow to you, the fourth, unmanifested reality indicated by the Supreme Consciousness, which we cannot recognise through our intelligence. That Being which is above all manifestation in the form of Sattva, Rajas, and Tamas properties and all the material form."

yaṁ dviṣyāt, asāv asmai kāmo mā samṛddhīti vā; na haivāsmai sa kāmaḥ samṛddhyate yasmā evam upatiṣṭhate; aham adaḥ prāpam iti vā.

Whatever you wish in your mind at the time of the chant of the Gayatri Mantra, that materialises itself.

Not only that; nobody can get what you can get. You stand above all people. You may prevent someone from getting something by the chant of the Gayatri, and you may get everything that you require by the chant of the Gayatri. Both things are possible.

The positive and the negative aspects of the power that accrues to one by the chant of Gayatri are mentioned here. You can oppose and prevent anything from taking place if it is not supposed to take place at all according to your will; or if it is to take place, it can take place also by your positive will. So, if you wish it should take place, it will; and if you wish it shall not, it will not.

Story 9 Story of Janak and a sage

एतद्ध वै तज्जनको वैदेहो बुडिलमाश्वतराश्विमुवाच
यन्नु हो तद्गायत्रीविदब्रूथा अथ कथꣳ हस्ती भूतो वहसीति ।
मुखꣳ ह्यास्याः सम्राण् न विदां चकारेति होवाच ।
तस्या अग्निरेव मुखं यदि ह वा अपि बह्विवाग्नावभ्यादधति
सर्वमेव तत्सन्दहत्येवꣳहैवैवंविद्
यद्यपि बह्विव पापं कुरुते सर्वमेव तत्सम्प्साय
शुद्धः पूतोऽजरोऽमृतः सम्भवति ॥ V.xiv.8 ॥

There is a peculiar story here. There was a sage called Buḍila Asvatarasvi. He was a reciter of the Gayatri Mantra, but he became an elephant in his next birth. Janaka was riding that elephant, and due to Purva Vasana the elephant could speak.

etadd ha vai taj janako vaideho buḍilam āśvatarāśvim uvāca: yan nu ho tad gāyatrī-vid abrūthāḥ, atha kathaṁ hastī bhūto vahasīti.

It said that it was a reciter of the Gayatri Mantra in previous birth. Janaka asked, "You say you are a meditator on Gayatri. How have you become an elephant upon which I am sitting and riding?"

mukhaṁ hy asyāḥ, samrāṭ, na vidām cakāra, iti hovāca;

The elephant said: "King, I did not know the mouth of Gayatri. I made a mistake in the chant. I did not know some aspect of it. I knew everything except something. That something has brought me to an elephant's birth."

tasyā agnir eva mukham:
yadi ha vā api bahu ivāgnau abhyādadhati,
sarvam eva tat saṁdahati;

"I see," said Janaka. "This is the case. Agni, Fire is her mouth. This you did not understand."

Perhaps the mouth is to be identified with the Sun himself, which is symbolic of the fire-principle.

Also, in the ritual of the chant of the Gayatri there are certain Nyasa, as they are called, placements which invoke Agni and other deities as the various limbs of the conceived body of the deity of Gayatri.

evaṁ haivaivaṁ-vid yady api bahv iva pāpaṁ kurute,
sarvam eva tat sampsāya śuddhaḥ pūto'jaro'mṛtaḥ sambhavati.

Just as anything that is thrown into fire is burnt to ashes, whatever it be, so does one burn to ashes every sin that one might have committed in the earlier births, provided one knows the secret of Gayatri in its entire form.

Agni as the Mukha and the fourth foot, particularly, must be understood.

We must meditate on Gayatri in its entirety and not part by part, and must also be able to identify the deity of the Gayatri as one with one's own being, united with one's own being, and with the chant which is Gayatri Mantra.

The Sadhana which is the Gayatri, the Sadhaka who is the meditator, and the deity, should all be contemplated as a single being. By this one attains to supernal regions.

The Gayatri Sadhana is again narrated in the story of Savitri and Satyavan. In the next chapter, we narrate Shakti as different parts of Prakriti, as per Upanishads and Puranas.

CHAPTER 13
PURANAS AND GODDESSES

Story 1: Important Puranas

The common practice of worshipping the divine mother is the worship of *Grama Devi*, the Goddess of the Village, is a very common practice in our villages. There are several stories related with these Goddesses told traditionally by village elders. Then, there are particular Devi worshipped more popularly in regional level. They, along with nationally worshipped Devis including Lakshmi, Sarasvati, Durga, Kali, Radha, and others are worshipped on special occasions, and fixed dates during in *Navaratri*, *Dashahara*, *Deepavali*, *Basanta Panchami*, *Sharad Purnima*, and so many other occasions.

Visiting fifty-one *Shakti Peethas* as a pilgrimage and worshiping there is a part in of the life of devotees of the Divine Mother.

Some Puranas where we have detailed stories about Goddesses are as follows:

1. Devi Bhagavata Purana

This Purana is dedicated entirely to the Goddess and includes extensive details about Durga and her various forms, including Kali. It discusses her birth, her battles against demons, and her significance in the cosmic order.

2. Markandeya Purana

The Markandeya Purana contains the **Devi Mahatmya** (also known as Durga Saptashati or Chandi Path), which narrates the story of Durga's battle against the buffalo demon Mahishasura. It is one of the most revered texts celebrating the Goddess and her divine powers.

3. Skanda Purana

This Purana includes stories about the Goddess Durga and her various manifestations. It elaborates on her divine roles and the rituals associated with her worship.

4. Linga Purana

The Linga Purana discusses the power of Shakti and includes references to Durga as a form of the divine feminine and emphasizes her role in the creation and preservation of the universe.

5. Brahmanda Purana

This text includes various myths and legends related to the Goddess and highlights her role as a protector of dharma as well as her fierce forms like Kali.

6. Vamana Purana

The Vamana Purana also mentions Kali in the context of her role as a fierce protector and embodies the power of destruction to restore cosmic order.

7. Brahm Vaivarta Purana

Various stories elaborate the Goddesses like Radha, Tulasi, Lakshmi, Ganga, and Saraswati

8. Sri mad Bhagavat Purana

This also include Ras Lila and other events,

Besides, almost all Puranas, and Tantras and Shakta texts elaborate on the worship of different Goddesses, emphasizing their significance in the Shakta tradition.

These Puranas and texts collectively portray the importance of different Goddesses as powerful, who embody strength, protection, and the triumph of good over evil. They highlight the importance of the feminine divine in Hindu cosmology and ritual practice.

Story 2: Important Goddesses in Puranas

· **Lakshmi:**

The goddess of wealth, fortune, and prosperity, usually depicted sitting on a lotus flower, often associated with Vishnu as his consort.

- **Saraswati:**

Goddess of knowledge, learning, music, and arts, often portrayed with a veena (stringed instrument) and a swan, considered the wife of Brahma.

- **Parvati:**

The motherly aspect of the divine feminine, wife of Shiva, often associated with fertility and creation, sometimes depicted as the fierce warrior goddess Durga when battling demons.

- **Durga:**

A powerful warrior goddess, often depicted with multiple arms wielding weapons, symbolizing the ability to overcome evil and protect devotees.

- **Kali:**

A fierce and sometimes terrifying form of Parvati, representing the destructive aspect of the divine, often depicted with a dark complexion, a garland of skulls, and a protruding tongue.

Story 3: Prakriti as Goddess

The prefix "Pra" in the word Prakriti means exalted, superior, excellent; and the affix "Kriti" denotes creation. So, the Goddess, the Devi Who is the most excellent in the work of creation is known as the Prakriti Devi.

To come closer: "Pra" signifies the Sattva Guna, the most exalted quality, "Kri" denotes the Rajo Guna and "Ti" denotes the Tamo Guna.

When this Intelligence of the nature of Brahm, beyond the three attributes, gets tinged with the above three Gunas and becomes omnipotent, then She is superior (Pradhan) in the work of creation. Hence, she is styled as Prakriti.

The state just preceding that of creation, the planning state, is denoted by "Pra"; and "Kri" signifies actual creation. So, the Great Devi that exists before creation is called Prakriti after creation.

The Paramatma by His Yoga Maya, divided Himself into two parts; the right side of which was male 'Purusha' and the left side was the female 'Prakriti'.

Prakriti is of the nature of Brahma. She is eternal. As the fire and its burning power are not different, so there is no separate distinction between Atman and His Shakti, between Purusha and Prakriti.

Prakriti is the Lady Controller of the Universe. Brahm is with Maya in a state of equilibrium.

Therefore, those that are foremost and the highest of the Yogis do not recognize any difference between a male and a female. All is Brahm. He is everywhere as male and female forever.

Atman and Prakriti are in inseparable union with each other. The union is like Fire and its burning capacity, the Moon and her beauty, the lotus and its splendor, the Sun and his rays.

As the goldsmith cannot prepare golden ornaments without gold and as the potter cannot make earthen pots without earth, so the Atman cannot do any work without the help of this omnipotent Prakriti.

The letter "Sa" indicates "Aishwarya" prosperity, the divine powers; and "Kti", denotes strength; and in as much as She is the bestower of the above two, the Mula Prakriti is named "Shakti".

"Bhaga" is indicative of knowledge, prosperity, wealth, fame; and in as much as Mula Prakriti has all these powers, she is also called "Bhagavathi".

And Atman is always in union with this Bhagavathi Who is all powers, so He is called "Bhagavan'. The Bhagavan is therefore sometimes with form; and sometimes He is without form.

Out of the Will of Shri Krisna, to create the world Whose Will is all in all, came out at once the Mula Prakriti, the Great Devi Ishwari. By Her command came out five Forms of Her, either for the purpose of creation or for bestowing Favors and Grace to the Bhaktas (devotees).

Story 4: Maha maya, or Durga

Parvati, the mother of Ganesha, comes, as the first, the most auspicious Goddess. She is loved by Shiva. She is also called Maha Maya, Narayani, Visnu Maya, and she is of the nature of Purna Brahma (the Supreme Brahma). This eternal, all auspicious

Devi is the Presiding Deity of all the Devas and is, therefore, worshipped and praised by Brahma and the other Devas, Munis, and all Jivas.

This Bhagvati Durga Devi, Ambika destroys all the sorrows, pains and troubles of the devotees that have taken Her refuge, and gives them Dharma, everlasting name and fame, all auspicious things and bliss and all the happiness, nay, the Final Liberation!

She is the Greatest Refuge of these Bhaktas that come to Her wholly for protection and are in great distress, whom She saves from all their dangers and calamities.

This Great Devi is the intelligence, sleep, hunger, thirst, shadow, drowsiness, fatigue, kindness, memory, caste, forbearance, errors, peace, beauty, and consciousness, contentment, nourishment, prosperity, and fortitude. She is sung in the Vedas and in other Shastras as the Maha Maya, Maha Lakshmi, and Maha Sarasvati.

She is of the nature of the Universe. In reality, she is the Adi-Shakti of the Universe and She is the Shakti of Krisna. All these qualities are also mentioned in the Vedas. Nobody can describe her properties, not even the different names by which she is called by the Vedas. She has infinite qualities.

We have narrated the stories of birth, Tapasya and marriage of Parvati with Shiva in second part of the series of books "Stories from Puranas" in detail. In the same part birth of Kartikeya, and Ganesha and Slaying of Tarakasurs, and Tripurasuras have also been narrated.

In first part of the series, the story of Dakshayani becoming Sati, and the Saktipithas has been narrated. We have also read the beautiful story of Vishnu killing Madhu and Kaitabh, with the help of Maha Maya in that book.

So, in this part we are narrating wonderful stories of Devi Durga manifesting from the combined energies of all Devas for killing Mahisasura. We will also narrate how Kaushiki and Kalika emerged from Parvati to end the reign of Shumbha and Nishumbha.

Story 5: Lakshmi

The second Shakti of the Paramatma is named Padma (Laksmi). She is of the nature of Shuddha Sattva (Higher than Sattva Guna) and is Vishnu's Presiding Deity of all wealth and prosperity.

This very beautiful Laksmi Devi is the complete master of the senses; She is of a very peaceful temper, of good mood and all-auspicious. She is free from greed, delusion, lust, anger, vanity and egoism.

She is devoted to Her husband and provider of immense happiness to Her Bhaktas. Her words are very sweet and She is very dear to Her husband, indeed, the Life and Soul of Him. This Devi is residing in all the grains and vegetables and so She is the Source of Life of all the beings.

She is residing in Vaikuntha as Maha Laksmi, chaste and always in the service of Her husband. She is the Heavenly Laksmi, residing in the Heavens and the royal Laksmi in palaces and the Grisha Laksmi in the several families of several householders.

All the lovely beauty that you see in all the living beings and all the things, it is She; She is the glory and fame of those that have done good and pious works and it is She that is the prowess of the powerful kings.

She is the trade of merchants, the mercy of the saints, engaged in doing good to others and the seed of dissensions in those sinful and vicious persons as approved of in the Vedas. She is worshipped by all, reverenced by all.

We are narrating some stories of mother Lakshmi in this book. Story of her manifestation during Churning of Sea has already been narrated in first part of the series. Also, the beautiful story in which she binds Rakhi to King Bali was narrated in that book.

Story 6: Sarasvati

The third Shakti of the Great God who is the Presiding Deity of knowledge, speech, intelligence, and learning, is named Sarasvati. She is all the learning of this endless Universe and She resides as Medha (intelligence) in the hearts of all the human beings.

She is the power in composing poetry; She is the memory and

She is the great wit, light, splendor and inventive genius. She gives the power to understand the real meaning of the various difficult Siddhanta works.

She explains and makes us understand the difficult passages and She is the remover of all doubts and difficulties. She acts when we write books, when we argue and judge, when we sing songs of music; She is the time or measure in music; She holds balance and union in vocal and instrumental music.

She is the Goddess of speech; She is the Presiding Deity in the knowledge of various subjects; in argumentations and disputations. In fact, all the beings earn their livelihood by taking recourse to Her. She is peaceful and holds in Her hands Vina (lute) and books.

Her nature is purely Sattvic (Shuddha Sattva), modest and very loving to Shri Hari. Her color is white like ice-clad mountains, like that of the white sandal, like that of the Kunda flower, like that of the Moon, or white lotus.

Story 7: Savitri

Savitri, or Gayatri is the other Devi in accordance with the Vedas. She is the mother of the four Varnas (castes), the origin of the (six) Vedangas (the limbs of the Vedas and all the Chhandas.

She is the Seed of all the mantras of Sandhya Vandana and the Root, the Seed of the Tantras; She Herself is versed in all the subjects. Herself an ascetic, she is the Tapas of the Brahmins.

She resides always in the Brahma Loka (the Sphere of Brahma) and is such as all the sacred places of pilgrimages want Her touch for their purification. She is called Ved Mata and also Chhand Mata.

Her color is perfectly white like the pure crystal. She is purely Shuddha Sattva, of the nature of the Highest Bliss; She is eternal and superior to all.

She is of the nature of Para Brahma and is the bestower of Moksha. She is the Fiery Sakti and the Presiding Deity of the Brahma Teja (the fiery spirit of Brahma, and the Brahmanas). The whole world is purified by the touch of the Savitri Devi.

We are going to narrate Savitri Devi in three of the chapters, one each from Veda, Upanishads, and Puranas.

Story 8 Radha

The Devi Radhika is the Fifth Sakti. She is the Presiding Deity of the five Pranas. She Herself is the Life of all; dearer than life even to Shri Krisna; and She is highly more beautiful and superior to all the other Prakriti Devis.

She dwells in everything. She is very proud of Her good fortune (Saubhagyam); Her glory is infinite; and She is the wife, the left body, as it were, of Shri Krisna and She is not in any way inferior to Him, either in quality or in the Tejas (Fiery Spirit) or in any other thing.

She is Eternal, of the nature of the Highest Bliss, fortunate, highly respected, and worshipped by all. She is, the Presiding Devi of the Rasa Lila of Shri Krisna. From Her has sprung the Rasa mandala and She is the Grace and the Ornament of the Rasa mandala (the dance in a circle in Rasa).

She is the Lady of the Rasa Lila, the Foremost of the Jovial, humorous (witty) persons and dwells always in Rasa. Her abode is in Goloka and from Her have come out all the Gopika.

Every female in every Universe is sprung from a part of Shri Radha or part of a part.

We have several stories of this Shakti in the book.

Story 9 The Ganges

Ganga has sprung from the lotus feet of Visnu. Her form is fluid-like. She is eternal. And She is the veritable burning fire to burn away the sins of the sinners. She is sweet to touch in taking baths and in drinking; She gives final liberation to the Jiva, and leads easily to the Goloka abode. She is the holiest amongst the places of pilgrimage and is the first of the running rivers.

She is the rows of pearls in the clotted hairs of Mahadeva's head. The Ganges purifies the three worlds and is the part of Mula Prakriti. She is pure Shuddha Sattva, clear, free from any Ahamkara, chaste and beloved of Narayana.

We have narrated the stories of Ganga emanating at the time of Ashvamedha Yagya of Raja Bali, Bhagirath bringing her for his ancestors, and Jahnu drinking her in the first part of the series.

In the second part, we have read stories of two sons of Ganga. Kartikeya taking birth in Ganga, and then Bhishma being the eighth surviving son of Ganga and Shantanu.

We are going to read another interesting story of Ganga in this book.

Durga and Kali are significant figures in several Puranas, particularly those that focus on Shakti (the divine feminine energy) and the various forms of the Goddess.

In the next chapters, we will read different stories from Puranas on important Goddesses. We start with Goddess Durga, Kali and other Matrikas. The first story is from Markandeya Purana, and Devi Bhagavat Purana.

CHAPTER 14
MAHISASURA

Story 1 Birth of Mahisa

Rambha and Karambha were the two sons of Danu, far famed in this world for their pre-eminence. They had no issues. Hence, desirous of issues, they went to the sacred banks of the Indus and there performed severe asceticism for long years.

Karambha then began his severe Tapasya being submerged in the water, while Rambha, had recourse to a juicy peepul tree, which was haunted by Yakshas and there remained, engaged in ascetic practices.

Knowing this, Indra was very anxious. He himself went to the place. He assumed the form of a crocodile and caught hold of the legs of the wicked Karambha and killed him.

Knowing this, Rambha got very much enraged. Wishing to offer his own head in Tapasya, he attempted to cut off his own head; holding the hairs of his head by his left hand, and, catching hold of a good axe, by his right hand.

Then the Agni, the fire god, appeared before him. He advised him to desist himself from this act and spoke, "You are stupid. Killing one's oneself is a great sin; and there is no means of deliverance from this sin. Do not seek your death now; rather ask boons from me. I will ensure your welfare."

Rambha desisted from his planned act. He said, "O Lord of the Devas! If you are pleased, grant my desired boon that a son be born to me, who will destroy the forces of my enemy and who will conquer the three worlds. And that son be invincible in every way by the Devas, Danava and men, very powerful, assuming forms at will, and respected by all."

The Fire god said, "O highly Fortunate! You will get your son, as you desire! With any female of whichever species, you will co-habit, you will get a son, undoubtedly more powerful than you."

Hearing this, Rambha went, surrounded by Yakshas, to a beautiful place, adorned with picturesque sceneries. Then one lovely she-buffalo, who was very maddened with passion, fell to the sight of Rambha.

As impelled by destiny, Rambha desired to have sexual intercourse with her. The she-buffalo, too, gladly yielded to his purpose and Rambha had sexual intercourse with her.

The she-buffalo became pregnant and Rambha carried the she-buffalo, as his dear wife, to Patala for her protection. After some times, a very powerful he-buffalo got excited for the she-buffalo. The Danava fought with the buffalo for the safety of his wife; whereon the excited buffalo killed him with his horns.

Seeing her husband dead, the she-buffalo quickly fled away in distress and, with terror, she quickly went to the peepul tree and took refuge under the Yakshas. But that buffalo, followed her, desiring intercourse with her.

The Yakshas assembled to fight and killed the buffalo. The Yakshas cremated the dead body of Rambha for its purification.

The she-buffalo, seeing her husband laid in the funeral pyre, entered into the burning fire along with her husband. When she died, her son rose from his mother's womb from the midst of the funeral pyre.

Rambha, too, emerged from the fire in a male form out of his affection towards his son. Rambha was known as Raktabija after emerging from fire in new form.

As per the boon of Agni, his son was born as a very powerful Danava and became famous by the name of Mahisa.

Story 2 Mahisasura becoming invincible

The chief Danava installed Mahisa on the throne. Mahisasura went to the mountain of Sumeru and performed a very severe and excellent Tapasya, wonderful even to the gods.

He continued meditation for full ten (thousand) years. Brahma, the grandfather of all the Lokas, was pleased with him. He arrived there on his vehicle, the swan, and asked Mahisasura, "O One of virtuous soul! Ask from me what is your desired object; I will grant you the boon."

Mahisa said, "O Lord, Lotus-eyed! I want to become immortal! please grant me the same so that I have no fear of death."

Brahma said, "O Mahisa! Birth must be followed by death, and death must be followed by birth; this is the eternal law of nature. Even that high mountains, vast oceans, along with all the living and non-living beings will die when time will come. Ask any boon other than this immortality; I will grant that to you."

Mahisa said, "O Grand Sire! Grant, then, that no Deva, Danava, nor human being of the male sex can cause my death. I am sure that there are no women who can cause my death. They are too weak to kill me! Therefore, O Lotus-eyed! Let woman be the cause of my death!"

Brahma said, "O Lord of the Danava! Your death will certainly occur, at any time, through a woman only. O Highly Fortunate One! No man will be able to cause your death."

Thus, granting him the boon, Brahma went to his own abode. The lord of the Danava, too, returned to his place, very glad.

The very powerful Danava Mahisa, thus became invincible by the Devas, Danava and human beings.

Story 3 Alternative story

As per Skanda Purana, the reason of Mahisasura getting the body of a buffalo was different. He was the son of Asura king Hiranyaksha, and was named Chitrasama. He was very handsome and valiant. He liked to ride buffaloes more than any other vehicle.

Once, he was engrossed in prey of water birds at the bank of Ganges. Sage Durvasa was meditating on the bank of river. Without seeing the sage, Chitrasama crossed him on his buffalo, injuring him very badly. This enraged the sage. He cursed, "As you are fond of riding buffaloes, your body also take the form of a buffalo."

Despite Chitrasama apologizing a lot, Durvasa left saying that he would have to suffer the curse. Then, he prayed Shukracharya, the Daitya guru. As per his advice, he prayed Mahadeva, and received the boon of invincibility, as stated above.

Story 4 Mahisa controls the world

The very powerful Asura Mahisa, puffed up with vanity on his getting the boon, defeated every king, and brought the whole world under his control! He, being the paramount power, began to rule the sea-girt earth acquired by the power of his own arms. His Commander-in-Chief was then the very powerful Chikshura, maddened with pride; and Tamra was in charge of the Royal Treasury, guarded by many soldiers. There were many powerful generals Asiloma, Vidala, Udarka, Vaskala, Trinetra, Kala, Bandhaka and others, very proud, and each in charge of his own corps respectively.

The powerful kings that reigned before were made subservient and tributary; and those, that fought valiantly befitting the Kshatriya line, were slain by Mahisa. The Brahmanas over the earth became subservient to Mahisa and gave their Yajna offerings to him.

Next, proud of his boons, he desired to conquer the Heavens. He sent an envoy to Indra. As ordered by him, the messenger and spoke to Indra fearlessly, "O thousand-eyed one! Quit the Heavens; go anywhere you like, or offer your service to the high-souled Mahisa! He is the lord; and if you take refuge unto him, he will certainly protect you. We know your powers. You were, in days of yore, conquered by our ancestors. Decide yourself! Give battle or go anywhere you like."

Hearing the messenger's words, Indra became very indignant and laughed and said, "I did not know, O you stupid, that you were maddened with vanity. I will shortly give medicines for your master's disease. Now I will extirpate him by the roots. Go and tell him 'If you are willing to fight, better come and do not delay. I will cut off your both horns and render you powerless. You are very much puffed up with vanity due to that.'"

The messenger quickly returned to his haughty master Mahisa

and saluting; he told everything that had been spoken by Indra. Hearing the messenger's words, the Danava got very angry and, waggling his tail behind his back, passed urine. Then his eyes reddened with anger, and he called the Danava chiefs before him.

He ordered them, "Go, and bring your forces. We will have to conquer that devil, the chief of the Suras. If hundreds and thousands of warriors like Indra come, I do not fear any of them at all. O Danava heroes, we will thoroughly put an end to him. His heroism is before those only that are peaceful and quiet like the ascetics that have become lean and thin by the penances."

"He is licentious and can only seduce other's wives by craftiness and arts. He is treacherous to his very core. Again, the powerful Visnu is a thorough master of treachery and hypocrisy. He can assume many forms at will by his Magic power. Never shall I surrender myself to Visnu, for I never place my trust in the words or deeds of Visnu and his Devas."

"Even the most powerful Rudra will not be able to fight against me in the battle-field because of Brahma's boon! I will instantly defeat them and get possession of their Heavens. On our conquering the Devas, we all shall get our share of Yajnas and enjoy ourselves in Heaven."

"O Chikshura! Call without any delay the chief Danava from the nether regions and the mountains and make them support me, although I can alone conquer all the Devas! I need all only to make the war arrangements look nice. There is no fear of mine from the Devas, consequent on the boon conferred on me."

"So, get yourselves ready to conquer the Devas. After conquering the Heavens, we will be garlanded with Parijat wreaths and we will enjoy the Deva women in the Nandana Garden. We will drink the milk of the heavenly milch cow (the cow that yields all desires) and, intoxicated with the heavenly drinks, we will hear and see the music and singing of the Gandharva's and the dancing of Apsaras there."

"Then be all ready at once for this auspicious occasion to march to Heavens and fight there with the Suras. And be pleased to call that pure-souled Muni Shukracharya, the son of Bhrigu and the Guru of the Daityas and worship him and tell him to perform rites and ceremonies for the safety and victory of the Danavas." Thus, ordering the chief Danavas, the wicked Mahisa went to his abode, with gladness.

Indra, on his part, called an assembly of Devas and addressed thus, "O Devas! the most powerful Mahisa, the son of Rambha, is now the king of the Danava. He has become haughty on the strength of his boon. O Devas! Mahisa has sent his messenger; he wants to attack and take possession of the heaven. He has asked to fight; or to surrender to him."

All the Devas decided to fight the Danavas. Deva guru Brihaspati was called, and he indicated bad times for Indra.

When the battle between two forces started, Indra was able to get support of Hari and Har also. However, despite initial setbacks, the Asuras were able to defeat the valiant Devas. Vishnu and Shiva created havoc among the rank of demons. However, they had to have to leave the battlefield after realizing the impact of boon of Brahma.

Even after Vishnu and Shiva left the battle-field, the Devas continued to fight under the leadership of Indra for long. But, finally the Danavas under Mahisasura were victorious, because he had the boon of invincibility against all men.

After the Devas were defeated by the lord of the Danavas, they were banished from heaven, their abode. While Danava now resided in Swarga, Devas were living in the caves of hills and dales. They were continuously attacked and oppressed by the Danavas. That wicked Danava king Mahis was thoroughly enjoying the heaven and also the share of the oblations of the Yajnas.

They were also enjoying the Airavata elephant, the Parijat tree and also the heavenly milch cow, Kamdhenu, and all the jewels of the ocean. They lorded over the Gandharva and Apsaras.

After vanquishing Devas, Mahisasura lorded over all three Lokas. His reign of terror over Devas and human was making everyone terribly sorry.

In next chapter, the manifestation of great Devi Durga, mother of all, is narrated.

CHAPTER 15
MANIFESTATION
OF MAHAMAYA

Story 1 Devas pray Shiva and Vishnu

The Devas headed by Indra, went to meet Brahma, the grandsire of the world. They said, "O Creator! O Lotus-born! How is it that you are not moved with pity towards the Devas, seeing and knowing everything of this world! O Lord! We lie prostrate at your feet. That vicious Danava, Mahisasura of wicked character and full of mischievous actions, gives us troubles in various ways wherever we go. Please help us!"

All the Devas, praising Him thus, bowed down and saluted him, with their faces very heavy, overladen with deep sorrow. Brahma consoled them with sweet words, and made them happy.

He said, "O Suras! What shall I do? The Danava can be killed by females only. O Suras! Let us all go to Kailash, take Shankara, the expert in doing the works of Gods, and go to Vaikuntha, where Visnu resides. There we all will unite and hold a counsel and decide what is best to do, to serve the purpose of the gods."

Deciding thus, Brahma riding on his Hamsa went to Kailash, accompanied by all the Devas. Shiva soon came out of his dwelling abode. When they met each other, they saluted each other and felt very glad. The Devas then bowed down to them. Shiva asked the welfare of Brahma and the Devas and asked the reasons of their coming to Kailash.

Brahma described the plight of Devas, and requested Shiva to find a way out.

Hearing thus, Sankara smiled a little and spoke, "O Bibhu! It is You that gave earlier this boon to Mahisa. Therefore, it is you that have wrought this mischief. Where can we get such a noble woman who becomes able to kill that Danava. My wife nor your wife ought to go to battle; even if they, how will they be able to fight? There is no lady who can kill this demon. I, therefore, propose to consult Visnu, foremost amongst the intelligent; and take actions after duly consulting with him."

Brahma and the other Devas accepted the proposal, and saying, "Be it so," all instantly rose up. At the time, seeing all the auspicious signs, they all became glad; and, riding on their respective vehicles, drove towards the abode of Visnu.

Soon the Devas reached Vaikuntha, and went to the golden palace of Hari, towering to heavens. There was the Divine Seat in the center, composed wholly of gems and jewels; and Visnu was occupying this seat.

Hari came up to them and seeing the Devas waiting at the doors very morose and tired, cheered them up by casting a favorable glance full affection and love. The gods bowed down and praised hymns to Jagannatha, the Deva of the Devas, and the enemy of the Daityas.

They said, "O Deva of the Devas! You are the Creator, Preserver and the Destroyer of the worlds! You are the ocean of mercy and the sole refuge of this Universe! O Lord! We have come to You as our Great Refuge. Do save us from the present difficulty. "

After being asked by Vishnu to narrate their cause, the Devas replied, "O Lord! The Asura Mahisa is very cruel and wicked; always addicted to vicious acts; now that most sinful Danava has become very much puffed up with pride and is tormenting us always. He is appropriating to himself the share of the Yajnas. We are therefore, terror-stricken and are wandering in mountains and fastnesses. He has become unconquerable due to his being granted the boon by Brahma."

"O Krisna! You are acquainted with all the tricks and Maya of the Daityas; therefore, you are capable to kill them. Therefore, be pleased! Devise means for that purpose. Where can we get a female who will be able to kill that demon in battle, and carry out the purpose of the gods."

Visnu on hearing their words, spoke smiling "We fought before; but this Asura could not at that time be killed because of the boon. Hence if some female Deity be now created out of the collective energy and form of the Sakti of each of the Devas, then that Lady would be able easily to destroy that Demon by sheer force, though he is skilled in hundreds of Mayas."

"Therefore, ask you all, with your wives respectively, boons from that portion which resides in you all in the form of Fiery Energy, that the collected energy thus manifested may assume the form of a Lady."

Story 2 Emission of Energy from all Devas

On Visnu, the Lord of the Devas, saying thus, came out spontaneously, at once, of the face of Brahma, the brilliant fiery energy, very difficult to conceive. That astonishing energy looked red like gems and pearls, hot, at the same time, a little cool, having a beautiful form, and encircled by a halo of light.

Next came out of the body of Sankara, His fiery spirit, quite in abundance and very wonderful to behold. It was silvery white, terrible, unbearable, and incapable of being seen even with difficulty. It extended like a mountain and looked horrible as if the incarnation of the Tamo Guna.

Next a dazzling light of blue color emanated from the body of Visnu. Thereafter, the light that came out of the body of Indra was hardly bearable, of a beautiful variegated color, and comprised in itself the three qualities.

Similarly, masses of lights came out respectively from Kubera, Yama, Fire and Varuna. The other Devas, too, gave their shares of fiery lights, very lustrous and splendid.

Story 3 Manifestation of Devi

Then these all united into a great Mass of Fire and Light. Like another Himalayan Mountain, the combined energy formed gigantic lustrous Divine light. Visnu and the other Devas were all extremely surprised to see this. While the Devas were thus looking steadfastly on that Fire, an exquisitely handsome Lady was born out of it, causing excitement and wonder to all.

This Lady was Maha Laksmi; composed of the three qualities of the three colors, beautiful, and fascinating to the universe. Her face was white, eyes were black, her lips were red and the palms of her hands were copper-red.

She was adorned with divine limbs and ornaments. The Goddess was now manifest with eighteen hands, though She had a thousand hands (in Her unmanifested state).

She became manifest out of the amalgamated mass of fire, and energy for the destruction of the Asuras. She sprung at the instant the word was spoken.

The Mahamaya is constant, and is always existent. Though She is one, yet She assumes different forms for the fulfilment of the Deva's ends, whenever their positions become serious.

The Nirguna Devi, Mahamaya, though formless, assumes many different forms of Sattvic, Rajasic or Tamasic qualities, to fulfil the Deva's purposes.

There are various names given to Her, according as the works done by Her vary immensely in their natures, just as the meanings of one root vary, some being principal and some secondary, according to the meanings and objects they convey.

Her grand beautiful white lotus-like face was created out of the fiery energy of Shankara. Her glossy black beautiful hairs of the head, overhanging to the knees, were formed out of the light of Yama.

Her three eyes came out of the energy of Fire. The pupils of those eyes were of a black color, the middle parts were of a white color and the ends were red. The two nicely curved eyebrows of the Devi were black and came out of the spirit of Sandhya. They were shedding, as it were, cooling rays.

From the light of Vayu (air), Her two ears were created, beautiful like the swinging seat (rocking chair) of the God of Love. Her nose was fashioned out of the energy of Kubera, the Lord of wealth, and was glassy and exquisitely charming.

Her pointed rows of glossy and brilliant teeth, looking like gems, came out of the energy of Daksa. Her lower lip was deep red and it came out of the fire of Aruna (the charioteer of the Sun). Her beautiful upper lip came out of the energy of Kartika.

Her eighteen hands came out of the energy of Visnu and Her red fingers came out of the energy of the Vasus. Her breasts came out of the energy of Soma and Her middle (navel) with three folds was created out of the spirit of Indra. Her thighs and legs were from Varuna and Her spacious loins came out from Earth.

Story 4 Vishnu asks all to adorn the Devi with jewels and Weapons

Thus, from the various lights and energies, contributed by the Devas, that Heavenly Lady came out. She was incomparably beautiful, and the voice was exquisitely sonorous and lovely.

The Devas, oppressed by Mahisasura, became overpowered with joy seeing this well decorated Devi, having beautiful eyes and teeth, and charming in all respects. Visnu then addressed all the Devas to give all their auspicious ornaments and weapons, endowed with strength, created out of their own weapons to the Devi.

Story 5 Devi gets auspicious ornaments and weapons

Then, the Kshirsagar (Milk Ocean) presented to her gladly, the well fitted necklace, clear as crystal, and a pair of divine cloths, of a red color, never becoming old and very fine.

Visvakarman presented a divine jewel to be worn in Her diadem or crest blazing like hundreds of suns; white earrings; bracelets for Her wrist, bracelets for Her upper arm, and other bracelets decked with various gems and jewels and anklets brilliant like gems, of a clear Sun-like luster, decked with jewels, and tinkling nicely. He gave Her as offerings beautiful ornaments also for the neck, as well as for the fingers decked with gems and jewels, all shining splendidly.

Varuna gave for Her head garland of lotuses, never fading away, of such a sweet fragrance as bees constantly hover round them and the Vaijayanti garland for Her breast. The mountain Himalaya gladly offered Her various gems and a beautiful lion, of a golden color for Her conveyance.

Then that beautiful Lady, having all the auspicious signs, wishing welfare to all, and decorated with the divine ornaments began to look grand and splendid, mounted on Her conveyance, the Lion.

Visnu then created another Sudarshan from His own Sudarshan Chakra, and offered it to Her. Shankara created another excellent Trisula from his own Trident, terrible and demon-killing, and offered it to the Devi. Varuna created another bright conch from his own conch and offered it gladly to the Devi.

Fire offered Her a weapon named Shataghni. Maruta offered Her a wonderful bow and arrow case filled with arrows. Indra created another dreadful thunderbolt from his own to offer her, and also gave the sonorous bell that used to hang from the elephant Airavata.

Yama, the God of Death, created another beautiful staff from his own scepter which takes away when time comes, the life of all beings. Brahma gladly gave Her a divine Kamandalu, pot filled with the Ganges water; and Varuna offered Her a weapon called Pasha.

Time gave Her an axe and a shield and Visvakarman gave Her a sharp Parasu. Kubera gave her a golden drinking cup, filled with Madhu; and Varuna offered Her a divine beautiful lotus.

Visvakarman gave Her the Kaumudi gada, whence hundreds of bells were hanging, an impenetrable armour and various other weapons. The Sun gave to the Divine Mother his own rays.

Story 6 Prayer by Devas

The Devas, seeing Her adorned with ornaments and weapons, began to praise and chant hymns to that most Auspicious Goddess, the Great Enchantress of the three worlds.

The Deva said, "Salutation to Shivaa, Salutation to the Most Auspicious! Salutation to you, the Bhagvati Devi! You are the Goddess Rudrani (the terrible), we always salute again and again to You. You are the Kala Ratri (the night of destruction at the end of the world)!"

"You are the mother! You are the success! You are the

intelligence, and the growth! You are the Vaishnavi! We salute again and again to You! We offer our salutations to that Supreme Cause, the Highest Goddess! You are within this Maya (the unborn) yet the Maya does not know You. O Mother! Do what is good to us!"

"Please overpower and kill the Mahisa. That demon is vulnerable by woman only, he is deceitful, cunning, dreadful, and swollen with pride on his having got the blessing. You are the only refuge of all of us. We are very much harassed and oppressed by the Danava; therefore, now protect us! We bow down to You."

Story 7 Goddess replies

When the Devas had praised thus, the Highest Goddess, the Giver of all happiness, then smilingly said in the following auspicious terms, "O Devas! Soon in the battle ground I will overpower that wicked Mahisa, of cruel disposition and take away his life."

Speaking thus in a melodious voice, the Supreme Goddess smiled and again said, "This world is all full of error and delusion. Really, it is very wonderful that Brahma, Visnu, Indra and other gods are all shuddering out of fear from Mahisa Danava. The power of Destiny is exceedingly great and terrible; its influence cannot be overcome even by the best of the Devas."

"The Time is the Lord of happiness and pain. Time is, therefore, the God. The wonder is this that even those who can create, preserve and destroy this world, they are being overpowered and tormented by Mahisa."

The Devi, thinking thus, smiled; then laughed and laughed very hoarsely. It seemed that a roar of laughter then arose.

The earth trembled at that extraordinary sound; the mountains began to move and the vast oceans that remained calm began to be agitated with billows. The uproar filled all the quarters and the mountain Meru trembled.

Then the Danava, hearing the tumultuous uproar, were all filled with tremendous fear and dread.

The Devas became very glad and said thus, "O Devi! Let victory be Yours; save us."

Next chapter is about a messenger sent by Mahisasura to ascertain the reason of noise, and him being sent back by Mahamaya.

CHAPTER 16 SPY AND MINISTER OF MAHISASURA

Story 1 Spy of Mahisa

The intoxicated Mahisa, hearing the uproar, became very angry, and struck with terror. He asked the Daityas "O Messengers! Go and ascertain how has originated this sound. Who has made this harsh sound? Bring that devil and I will kill that roaring villain, who, it seems, has been puffed with egoism and vanity. The Devas are not making this noise, for they are vanquished and terror-stricken. The Asuras are not doing so, for they are my subjects. Then, who is the stupid fellow that has done so?"

No sooner the messengers heard these words of Mahisa, than they at once went to the place where Goddess was seating. They saw the beautiful and auspicious Goddess. She was holding excellent divine weapons.

She was holding in Her hands, the cup and drinking Madhu (Honey) again and again. Beholding Her this form, they were afraid and fled at once to the Mahisa and informed him the cause of that sound.

The Daityas said, "O Lord! We have seen one grown up woman; whose whereabouts we are quite ignorant. The Devi is decorated with jewels and ornaments all over her body. She is not human nor Asuri. Her form is extraordinary and beautiful. That noble Lady is mounted on a lion, holding weapons on all Her eighteen hands and is roaring loudly."

"She is drinking wine. It is quite certain that She has no husband. The Devas are gladly chanting praises from the celestial space that Let Victory be to Her side and that She save the Devas. O Lord! We are very much overpowered by the halo emitted from Her; and we could not even see Her well."

"O King! In compliance with your order, we have come back to you no sooner we had seen the lady, without even addressing her in any way. Now order us what we are to do."

Story 2: Mahisasura sends his Prime minister

Mahisa then asked his prime minister, "O Hero! Under my command, go there with all the forces and use the means, conciliation, etc., and bring that woman, adopting the three policies, Sama (conciliation), Dana (making gifts), and Bheda (sowing dissensions in her group)."

"And if all fail, then apply the last resort Danda, (or punishment) in such a way that her life be not destroyed and bring that beautiful woman to me. I will gladly make her my queen-consort, as I am enchanted on hearing about Her beauties and wealth."

The prime minister, on hearing the words of Mahisasura, took with him soldiers on elephants, horses, and chariots and hurriedly went to the desired place. On coming near to the Devi, the minister began to address her in sweet words from a sufficient distance in a very humble and courteous way.

He said, "O Sweet speaking! Who are you? What has caused you to come here? O Highly fortunate! My master has conquered all the Lokas (worlds). On account of getting his boon from Brahma, he is invincible, and assumes different forms at will. He, our King Emperor Mahisa, the lord of the earth, hearing about your beauty and dress, has expressed a desire to see you. Be pleased now to go to that intelligent King."

"In case you do not go, we will bring the King, your devotee, to you. We will therefore do exactly what You desire. Therefore, O beautiful lady! Be pleased to express what you desire and we will obey your orders."

Then Maha Maya, hearing thus the words of the prime minister of Mahisasura, laughed a lot.

She spoke with a voice, deep like that of a cloud, thus," O Minister-in-chief! Know me as the mother of the gods. My name is Maha Laksmi. I am requested by all the Devas to kill Danava Mahisasura; who has oppressed and deprived them of their share of Yajna offerings. Therefore, I have come here today alone, without any army to take away his life."

"O Good One! I am pleased with your sweet words of welcome, in showing me marks of respect. Otherwise, I would have certainly burnt you to ashes by my fiery sight."

"O Minister! Go you to Mahisa and speak to him the following words of mine, 'O Villain! Go down to Patala (the nether regions) at once if you have any desire to live. Otherwise, I will slay you, the wicked one, in the battle-field! O Asura! Or if you desire to fight, then come at once with your powerful warriors, and I will destroy all of them. Go to Patala, or anywhere else you like.'"

Hearing these words of the Devi, that minister, replied in reasonable words thus, "O Devi! You are speaking in words not befitting a woman, being puffed up with pride. You are a woman; the lord of the Daityas is a hero; how can a battle be engaged between you two. It seems to me impossible."

"Your body is delicate, a girl in full youth; and you are alone. Mahisa is of huge body and powerful; and has armies of elephants, horses, chariots, infantry, etc., and countless soldiers all armed with weapons. He will find no difficulty in killing you in battle."

"Rather, if I utter anything harsh to you, that would go against the sentiment of love that he feels for you. If I speak rudely to you, it will go against his feeling. Our king has become extremely devoted to you on hearing your extraordinary beauty. So, I must speak sweet words to you for the sake of pleasing my master."

"O Large-eyed! This kingdom and the wealth thereof are all yours. In fact, Mahisa will be your obedient servant. Therefore, better forsake your anger, leading to your death; and cultivate friendship with him. I am falling at your feet, and request you better go to him and become at once queen-consort. Then, you will get all the pure wealth of the three worlds and the unbounding happiness of this world."

The Devi said, "Minister! I now speak what is pregnant with goodness and wisdom to you, according to the rules of the Shastras, keeping in view also the cleverness that you have shown in using your words. Since you are the chief secretary of Mahisa, your nature and intelligence are like those of a beast."

"Did you think a little beforehand the meaning of your words when you told me of my feminine nature? Though I am not apparently a man, yet my nature is that of the Highest Purusha (Man); I shew myself simply in a feminine form to fulfil the boon of Brahma."

"Now see that your master Mahisa has shown his intelligence, when he courted his death from the hands of a woman. For that very reason, I have come here in the shape of a woman. He should not think simply on the strength of him getting some boons "that he would never die."

"Therefore, go quickly to your king and speak to him that I have said. If he wants his life, he, with his retinue, would at once go down to Patala. If he holds a contrary opinion, let him be eager to go to the house of Death and come and fight with Me."

Story 3: Danava Prime Minister thinks and returns

Hearing these words of the Devi, the Danava began to think whether to fight or to go to Mahisa?

Finally, he thought, "I ought not to fight here rashly; for victory or defeat would alike be distasteful to my monarch. Whether this Lady kills me, or I kill her, the king will be angry in either case. I will therefore go now to the king and tell him what the Devi has said; he will do whatever he likes."

Thus, that intelligent minister argued and went to the king. Then, bowing down before him, he began to say thus, "O King! That excellent woman, fascinating to the world, the beautiful Devi is sitting on a lion with weapons in all her eighteen hands. O King! I told her to choose to make Mahisa your husband, you will become fortunate amongst women and will enjoy ever all the wealth of the three worlds."

He then informed that that large-eyed woman, puffed up with egoism, laughed a little and said thus, "Your king is born of a buffalo and is the worst of brutes. Is there any woman in this world so stupid as to select Mahisa as her husband? O You stupid! I will fight and destroy the enemies of the gods in the battle-field. Or if he desires to live, let him flee to Patala."

He furthered told, "O King! Hearing those rough words uttered by Her in a moment of madness, I have returned to you. I did not fight with Her; especially, without Your command, how can I engage myself in useless excitement?"

"O Lord of the Earth! That handsome woman rests maddened on Her own strength. I do not know what is in the womb of future. Whatever is destined to happen, will surely come to pass. You are the sole master in this matter; I will do whatever you order me. The matter is very difficult to be reflected upon; whether it is better to fight or it is better to fly away, I cannot say definitely."

The King Mahisasura was not happy hearing these words. He, maddened with pride, then called the aged and experienced ministers for counsel.

CHAPTER 17
MEETINGS WITH MINISTERS.

Story 1 First meeting with counsellors

Mahisasura said to his ministers, "O Ministers! What am I to do now? Better judge you all well, and speak out definitely to me. You are all dexterous and therefore you would better tell me which course, we are to adopt now."

The ministers said, "O King! One should always speak true and at the same time pleasant. O King! As a medicine, though bitter, cures diseases, so true words, though appearing unpleasant, lead to beneficial results. Those that are simply pleasant, are generally injurious as to their effects. How can we then definitely pronounce our judgment in this difficult matter?"

The King said," Let each of you say separately, according to his own intellect, what is his opinion. I will hear them all and consider for myself. Clever persons should hear the opinions of several persons, then judge for himself what is the best and then adopt that as what is to be done."

The powerful Virupaksa came out foremost of all and began to say pleasant words to the King, "O King! Please take for certain, what has been spoken by that ordinary woman, swelled with vanity, as words simply to scare you. O King! You have conquered the three worlds by your own heroic valor. Now if you acknowledge your inferiority, out of fear to a woman, you would be subject to very much disgrace in this world."

"Therefore, O King! I will go alone to fight with Chandika and I will tie her down by a coil of snakes and bring before you. Then that Lady, seeing herself helpless, will become quite submissive to you; there is no doubt in this."

Another minister Durdhara said, "O King! Virupaksa is very intelligent. What he has said just now is all reasonable and true. O King! Please hear my words full of truth also. As far as I think, I consider that woman with beautiful teeth as passionate. She has expressed a desire to bring you under control by making you fearful. The mistresses, proud of their beauty generally use such words when they become passionate to attract dear persons towards them."

"O King! That woman has said, "I will pierce and kill you by arrows, face to face, in the battlefield." The sense of this is different. You can easily see that the handsome women have no other arrows with them; their side glances are their arrows. She actually said, "O Stupid! I will kill your King by my arrow-like eye-sight." But the messenger was wanting in that power to appreciate."

"The saying of that lady, "I will lay your lord in the death-bed in the battle-field" is to be taken in the light of inverted sexual intercourse, where woman is above the man. Her utterance, "I will take away the vitality (life) of your lord" means that she will make you devoid of your virility. There can be no other meaning. O King! The experts only in these amorous affairs will be able to appreciate these things. Knowing thus, dealings ought to be made with Her so that the harmony in amorous sentiments be not broken."

"O King! Sama (conciliation) and Dana (gifts) are the two means to be adopted; there is no other way. By these two, that Lady, whether she be proud or angry, is sure to have brought under control. I will go now and bring Her before you by such sweet words."

But their view was completely opposed by the Danava Tamra, who was very experienced in finding out the real nature. He said, "I am telling you what is sanctioned by virtue. This intelligent woman is not at all passionate nor devoted to you, nor has that woman used any covert expressions to you. O Great Hero! A good-looking woman, powerful, and having powerful weapons in eighteen hands is never heard of, nor ever seen by me in these three worlds. O Lord! This woman is neither human, nor a Gandharvi, nor the wife of any Asura. It is Maya of Devas."

"But in no case, weakness is to be resorted. It is wise by all means to fight as best as possible; what is inevitable will come to pass. This is my opinion. O King! Life or death is at the hands of Destiny; Nobody, therefore, can do it otherwise.

Hearing these unpleasant words, Mahisasura was angry on Tamra. He said, "O Highly fortunate Tamra! Better, then, stand for fight, fully resolved and conquer her according to rules of justice and bring her before me. In case She does not come under your control in fight, kill her. But if She comes round, then show her honor; do not kill her."

He ordered Tamra to go to Devi with a mighty force and find out her intention, and origin beforehand; and then fight with her without showing any weakness, or merciless behavior.

Story 2 Tamra goes and comes back alive

Thus, hearing the King's words, Tamra coming as if under the sway of Death, saluted the king Mahisa and marched away with his army. He began to see all the fearful inauspicious signs, indicative of Death. He became surprised and was caught with fear.

When he arrived at the spot, he saw the Devi standing on a lion, decorated with all the weapons and instruments.

Tamra, then bowed down before Her with humility and modesty and addressed Her with sweet words, according to the rules of the policy of conciliation. "O Devi! Mahisasura, the lord of the Daityas, has become enchanted on hearing Your beauty and qualifications and has become desirous to marry You. O Beautiful One! Make him your husband and enjoy all the exquisite pleasures of the heaven as best as you can."

"The end and aim of attaining this human form, beautiful in every respect and the abode of all bliss, is to enjoy, in every way, all the pleasures of human existence and to avoid the sources of all troubles. This is the rule."

"O beautiful! Your soft and delicate lotus-like hands are fit to play only with nice balls of flowers. Why then are You holding in Your hands all the weapons and arrows? The war is exceedingly painful in this world; those who know thus ought never to fight. It is only those human beings that are prompted by greed that fight with each other."

"O Delicate One! Gladly you can worship Mahisa, the lord of the world and the object of worship of the Devas and Danava. Then he will satisfy all your desires, as his queen-consort. Accept my request, you will surely get all the best pleasures. If you marry Mahisa, you will have beautiful sons and those sons again will be kings; and you will no doubt, be happy in your old age also."

The Goddess, hearing Tamra's words, spoke laughing a little and with a deep voice like that of a rumbling thunder cloud.

The Devi spoke, "O Tamra! Go and say to your Lord Mahisa who, it seems, is stupid, whose end is nigh, who has become very passionate, and who is void of knowledge what is proper and what is improper. I am not like your grown-up mother, the she-buffalo, having horns, eating grass, with a long tail and a big-belly."

"I am not desirous of any more husband. My Husband is existing. Though He is the Lord of all, Witness of All, yet He is not the Actor. He is without any desires and He is calm and tranquil. He, the Shiva, is devoid of any Prakriti qualities, and without any attachment. He is the abode of all, capable to do all, and He is seeing everywhere. How can I then leave Him and try to serve the dull, stupid Mahisa?"

"See! The combination of similar substances leads to happiness; and if out of ignorance, the connection takes place between things entirely different in their natures, it becomes at once the source of all pains and troubles. Do you not see me endowed with exquisite beauty? and what is your Mahisa? A buffalo with horns! Better fly away or fight if you like!"

Thus saying, the Devi howled and roared so loudly that it

appeared strange and it caused a great terror to the Danava. Tamra was terrified; his mind became unsteady and he at once fled to Mahisa.

The Danava present in the city became deaf; thy fled and became very anxious and were absorbed in the thought whence and how that sound came. The lion, too, enraged and, raising up its manes, roared so loud that the Daityas became very much terrified.

Story 3: Second round of counselling

Mahisa, too, became confounded to see Tamra returning. He then again held a council with his ministers what ought to be done next?

Mahisasura said, "O best of the Danava! Shall we now take our shelter within the forts? Or shall we go out and fight? Or should we fly away? Consult over the matter in utmost privacy and in strictest confidence amongst the good and virtuous ministers. If the plan be out, then destruction comes both to the King and his Kingdom."

"First find out the cause why this powerful woman, created by the Devas has come here alone and helpless? Victory or defeat lies at the hands of the Luck and Destiny. Is there anyone who has seen Fate? Therefore "effort," "energy" are the words of the heroes and "Fate" is the word of the cowards."

"You should all consider today these subjects fully and intelligently and then decide what are we to do? O Ministers! Then declare, taking due consideration of time and place, after duly discussing and ascertaining what is the best course to adopt, what would be beneficial and full of reason and intelligence."

Hearing this, the famous Vidalaksha with folded hands spoke thus, "O King! First it should be definitely ascertained whose wife is she, this woman possessing large eyes? Whence and for what purpose has she come here? Next what ought to be done should be decided."

"It seems to me that the Devas, knowing that your death will ensue from the hands of a woman, have created very carefully this lotus-eyed woman out of their own essences. When the war will ensue, Visnu and the other Devas will put this woman in front and slay us all. Whereas this Devi will slay you. This is their earnest desire."

"O King! Even after knowing this, the duty of your servants lies in this: -- That we should sacrifice at any moment our lives for the preservation of your prestige and to enjoy with you whenever you are enjoying. So, ponder over this very carefully when we see that this woman, though alone, is challenging us to fight who are armed with powerful soldiers."

Durmukha said, "O King! I know for certain, that we will not get victory in this battle. Still, we ought not to show our backs; for that would lead us to sheer disgrace. Therefore, fight we must; that is certain; let whatever happen. If we die in the battle, we will get name and fame; if we be victorious, we will get happiness. Thus, thinking both the cases, we must fight today."

Hearing this, Vaskala, the eloquent speaker, thus spoke to the king, with clasped hands and his head bowed down, "O King! You need not think thus in agony with this unpleasant affair. Alone I will kill that Chandika, of unsteady eyes. I will kill Her with these arrows, sharpened on stones. You can see today the prowess of my arms and enjoy peace; you will not have to go to battle anymore to fight with Her."

Durdhara, the commander of forces, now bowed down and said thus, "O Lord of the earth! Let the purpose be whatsoever, with which the beautiful Devi with eighteen hands, the creation of the gods, may come hither, I will vanquish Her. O King! I think, it is simply to terrify you. Know this merely as a scare."

"O King! Never put your trust on ministers. If you do so, they will always hinder you in your actions and counsels. What harm cannot be done by those ministers that are treacherous, greedy, deceitful and void of any intelligence and always addicted to vicious acts, when they are trusted!"

"Therefore, O King! I will go myself to the battle and serve your purpose. Let you be calm; and look at my strength, fortitude and valor."

CHAPTER 18 SLAYING OF VASKALA AND DURMUKHA

Story 1 Killing of Vaskala
The two powerful Danava Vaskala and Durmukha, well-versed in arts of warfare, went out for battle, maddened with their prowess. They began to address the Devi in voice deep as the rumbling of a cloud.

They said," O Beautiful Devi! You better choose and worship the Lord of the Daityas, that high-souled Mahisasura who has conquered all the Devas. He will come before you in privacy in a human shape, with all auspicious signs and adorned with beautiful ornaments. If you select him as your husband, you will be the mistress of those incomparable worldly happinesses that women always aspire."

Hearing these words of Vaskala and Durmukha, the Devi said, "O Stupid! Do you think me as deluded by passion? Do I not possess strength and intelligence that I will worship that hypocrite Mahisa as husband? How can a Devi, becoming passionate, worship the worst of all beasts, the beast Mahisa?"

"O two Asuras! Go back immediately to your King Mahisa resembling in his body like an elephant and having a pair of horns and tell him, go either to Patala (the nether regions) or come and fight with Me. O Beast! Without conquering Me, you would get no shelter either in the heavens, or in this earth, or in the caves of mountains?"

Hearing thus, the two powerful Daityas, with eyes reddened with anger, firmly resolved to fight and took bows and arrows in their hands.

The Devi then made a terrible noise and fearlessly stood there. The two Danava then began to shoot dreadful arrows at Her. For the victory of the Devas, the Devi also begin to hurl arrows after arrows on the two Danava, emitting a sweet sound.

Vaskala first came forward without further delay; and Durmukha stood aloof there simply as a witness. The terrible fight then ensued between the Devi and Vaskala. Arrows, swords and weapons were seen shining in the air and raised terror to all.

Then the mother of the Universe seeing Vaskala growing turbulent shot at him five arrows sharpened on stone. The Danava, too, cut off the arrows of the Devi and hurled seven arrows at her, seated on a lion.

The Devi cut off the Danava's arrows and shot at that hypocrite, sharpened arrows and began to laugh frequently. She again cut off his arrows with half-moon shaped arrow. Vaskala then pursued the Devi with a club in his hands to slay Her.

Seeing the arrogant Danava with club in his hands, Chandika Devi struck him down on the ground with her own club. The very powerful Vaskala fell down on the ground but rose up within a very short time and hurled again on the Devi his club.

Seeing him again attacking Her, the Devi got angry and pierced him with Her trident; Vaskala fell down, thus pierced, and died.

Story 2: Durmukha slayed by Devi

On Vaskala being slain, Durmukha came forward on the battle-field, filled with anger and accompanied by a stronger army. He was mounted on a chariot, and had shielded all over his body with a coat of armor.

He came before the Devi, with bows and arrows in his hands, shouting all along, "Wait, wait, O weak woman!"

The Devi blew Her conch shell and made large sounds by stretching Her bow. This made the Danava infuriated with anger. He then began to shoot sharp arrows after arrows like poisonous snakes.

The Mahamaya, by Her own arrows, cut off those of Her enemy and began to shout loudly. The fight then raged furiously, when both parties began to use arrows, Sakti, clubs, Masalas, and Tomaras.

Blood began to flow in the battle-field in torrents like rivers and on the banks of that river of blood, were seen the severed heads of the dead bodies which looked like so many hollow shells of gourds, as if kept there by the attendant of the god of Death, for their swimming purposes.

The battle-field, then, became very dreadful and impassable. Air began to emit an offensive smell, because of its contact with these corpses. It was very noisy as there were heard the heart-rending sounds of various carnivorous birds and animals.

Then the wicked Durmukha began, as if inspired by the god of Death, to address the Devi angrily and arrogantly with his right hand raised up before Her, "Your brain has become perverted! O Devi, fly away just now or I will send you unto death, or you better accept Mahisa, the lord of the Daityas, as your husband."

The Devi said, "O Villain! I see your death at hand this very day. Therefore, you are deluded and therefore raving like a mad man. I will kill you today like Vaskala. O Stupid! Better fly away; or if you prefer death, then wait! I will slay you first; then the dull Mahisa, the son of a she-buffalo."

Hearing thus, Durmukha, as if prompted by Death, hurled dreadful arrows on the Devi. Instantly the Devi, too, cut off all his arrows and, infuriated with anger, pierced the Danava by sharpened arrows. The fight then turned out very dreadful.

Instantly the Devi cut off the Asura's bow and broke his chariot by five arrows. On seeing his chariot broken, the powerful Durmukha attacked on foot the Devi with his club, very hard to overcome.

He knocked at the head of the lion with that club with great force; but the powerful lion did not become unsteady, though so very hard hit.

Seeing the demon thus standing before Her, the goddess Ambika cut down his head by her sharpened axe. On his head being thus severed, Durmukha fell down dead on the field.

The band of Devas, then, loudly shouted, "Victory to the Devi."

The Rishis, Siddhas, Gandharva, Vidyadhara, and Kinnaras all became very glad to see the Demon dead on the field.

Hearing the death news of Durmukha, Mahisasura became blind with anger and began to utter repeatedly to the Danava, "O! What is this? What is this? Alas! That delicate woman has slain in battle the two heroes Durmukha and Vaskala! what are we to do hereafter? You all judge and say what is reasonable at this critical juncture."

CHAPTER 19 SLAYING OF CHIKSHURA AND TAMRA

Story 1 Chikshura attacks and laid senseless

Then, his general Chikshura, the great warrior spoke as follows, "O King! Why are you so anxious as to take away the life of a delicate woman? I will kill her."

After consoling Mahisasura in this way, he himself departed for battle, mounted on his chariot and accompanied by his own army. The powerful Tamra accompanied him as his attendant; with his own army.

All the quarters became filled with the clamor of their vast army. Seeing them before her, Devi made an extraordinary wonderful sound with Her conch shell, with Her bow string and with Her great bell.

The Asuras heard that and trembled and fled, speaking amongst each other, "What is this?"

The Chikshura seeing them turning their backs, told them very angrily, "O Danava! What fear has now overcome you? I will slay today this vain woman in the battle with arrows. So, you should quit your fear and remain steady in battle."

Thus saying, he came fearlessly before the Devi with bows and arrows in his hands and, accompanied by his army, angrily spoke thus, "O Thou of large and broad eyes! Why are you roaring to terrify the weak persons! I have heard all about your deeds. But I am not a bit afraid of You."

"O Beautiful One! I have never heard a woman like you coming to fight with arms and weapons. Oh! Who can praise that Dharma which allows this dear body of ours to be pierced by sharpened arrows?"

"This dear body is nourished by sweet food, by being smeared with oil, and by smelling the scents of beautiful flowers. Ought, then, one to destroy it by arrows from an enemy? O beautiful! What merits have you found in the battle that you have chosen this. It is only those cunning poets that praise these; they say that those who die in battle go to heaven!"

Replying the Danava, the Divine Mother addressed him thus, "O Stupid! Why are you speaking false words, having no significance, like a literary man giving out mere words only? You do not know anything of politics, ethics, metaphysics. You do not know what are the royal duties; then what are you speaking before me?"

"I will kill that Mahisasura in battle, thus establish firmly my pillar of fame and then go happily to my abode. O Stupid! Better go to Patala with all the Danava, if you and Mahisa desire to live any longer. And if you like to go unto death, then be ready and fight without any delay. I will slay you all; this is my firm resolve."

Hearing the Devi's words, the Danava, proud of his own strength, began to hurl instantly on Her showers of arrows, as if another shower of rain burst upon Her. The Devi cut off those arrows into pieces by Her sharp arrows and shot at him dreadful arrows like poisonous snakes.

Then their fight became astounding to the public; the Divine Mother, then, struck him with Her club so hard that he fell down from his chariot. That vicious demon, thus struck by the club, remained senseless near to his chariot for two muhurtas, fixed like a mountain.

Story 2: Tamra joins the fight

Tamra, the tormentor of the foes, seeing him thus, could not remain steady and came forward to fight with Chandika.

The Devi seeing him laughed and said, "O Danava! Come! Come! I will instantly send you unto death. Or, what is the use of your coming? You are so weak that you can be called lifeless. No use in killing you, if that wicked Mahisa, the enemy of the gods, be not slain."

Hearing Her words, Tamra became very angry and drawing his bow up to his ear, began to hurl arrows after arrows on Chandika Devi. The Bhagvati, too, had her eyes reddened with anger and drawing Her bow began to shoot arrows quickly at the demon, wishing to kill, as early as possible, the enemy of the gods.

In the meanwhile, Chikshura regained his senses, and taking up again his bow in an instant, came before the Devi. Then Chikshura and Tamra, the two valiant warriors, began to fight dreadfully with the Devi.

Mahamaya then, became very angry and began to hurl arrows after arrows so incessantly that all the armors of all the Danava became pierced and were cut down to pieces. The Asuras, thus pierced by arrows, became infuriated with anger and hurled angrily a network of arrows upon the Devi.

Story 3: Both slayed

Tamra struck on the head of the lion with his dreadful hard Musala (club), made of iron, and laughed and shouted aloud.

Seeing him thus vociferating, the Devi became angry and

cut off his head by her sharp axes in no time. The head being thus severed from the body, Tamra, though headless, for a moment turned round his Musala and then fell down on the ground.

The powerful Chikshura, seeing Tamra thus falling down, instantly took up his axe and ran after Chandika. Seeing Chikshura with axe in his hand, the Bhagvati quickly shot at him five arrows. With one arrow, his axe was cut down, with the second arrow his hands were cut and with the remaining ones his head was severed from his body.

Thus, when the two cruel warriors were slain, their soldiers soon fled away in terror in all directions.

The Devas were exceedingly glad at their downfall and showered gladly flowers from the sky and uttered shouts of Victory to the Devi, "O Goddess! Victory, victory be Yours."

CHAPTER 20 ASILOMA AND VIDALAKSHA

Story 1 Asiloma and Devi discuss philosophy

Hearing the two mighty demons slain by the Devi, Mahisasura became very much amazed and sent the powerful Asiloma and Vidalaksha and the other Danavas to the battle to kill the Devi. The Danavas, all very skilled in the art of warfare, marched on for battle, fully equipped with weapons and clad in armour, and attended by a vast army. They arrived there and saw the Divine Mother with eighteen hands taking her stand on a lion, with axes and shield in her hands.

The calm-tempered Asiloma appeared before the Devi ready to kill the Daityas, saluted Her and smilingly said, "O Devi! Why have You come here? and what for You are killing these faultless Daityas? O Beautiful One! Tell all these to me truly. We will make treaty with you. Your body is very delicate. Why do you bear the stroke of weapons on your body? Happiness is only to be had and pain is to be avoided; this is the rule."

"If you follow the opinion of the Mimamsakas and do not believe in the existence of future births, even then you ought not to fight. When you have got this youthful age, you ought to enjoy the excellent pleasures in this world. And if you accept in the existence of the other worlds after death, even then you ought to desert from fighting and perform, in this life, such actions as will lead you to the attainment of Heavens."

"O Mother! Why are you killing these Daityas without any cause? Have the feeling of mercy! The sages always preserve piety, mercy and Truth. O Beautiful One! Then what is the use in Your killing these Demons? Please say explicitly on this point."

The Devi said, "O Powerful one! Hear why I have come here and why I am killing the Daityas? O Demon! I, though merely a spectator, always go about all over the worlds, seeing the justices and injustices done by the several souls there."

"Never I possess any desire of enjoyment, nor have I greed for anything, nor have I enmity with any creature. Only to preserve the virtue and religion and to keep up the righteous, I roam over the worlds. This is My vow and I always adhere to it."

"I incarnate Myself in yugas after yugas. Now the wicked Mahisa is ready to destroy the Devas; seeing this, I have come here to kill him. Knowing this, you remain or depart, as you desire. Or you can go to Mahisa, and say what is the use in sending other Asuras to the battle; he can come himself and fight."

Story 2: Asiloma and Vidalaksha discuss, decide to fight

Hearing thus the Devi's words, Asiloma asked gladly, before the Devi, the powerful Asura Vidalaksha, "Well, Vidalaksha! You have heard just now all what the Devi has said. Decide now, are we to observe treaty or declare war. What are we to do under the circumstances?"

Vidalaksha said, "Our king knows fully well that his death will certainly take place in the battle; knowing this, he is not willing to make peace, out of his egoism and vanity. He is seeing before him daily the deaths of the Danava and still he has sent us to battle."

"Who can overcome the destiny? The duty of a servant is a very difficult one; he will have to be always submissive and obedient, without caring the least for his own self-respect."

"How can we then go to our master and say such hard words as he would give away to the Devas all the gems and jewels and go down to Patala with other Danava. True and at the same time beneficial words are very rare in this world. At such critical cases, one ought to remain silent. Therefore, we ought to consider our lives as nothing and to fight for our king are what is best for us."

Thus, discussing among themselves, the two heroes then wore their coats of armor, mounted on their chariots and, with bows and arrows in their hands, became ready for fight.

Story 3: End of both mighty Asuras and the force

First the great warrior Asiloma stood aloof at a distance as a mere witness, letting Vidalaksha attack.

Vidalaksha shot seven arrows. The Divine Mother cut off those arrows to pieces with Her arrows, no sooner they reached Her, and then shot at Vidalaksha three arrows sharpened on stone.

The demon Vidalaksha had fallen senseless by these arrows on the battlefield and after a short while died, as if ordained by Fate. Seeing Vidalaksha thus dead, Asiloma took up his bows and arrows and came up, for fight.

The hero, then, raising his left hand, said briefly, thus, "O Devi! I know that death is inevitable to the Danava. Still I am ready to fight, for I am dependent on Mahisa, who is of very dull intellect. He cannot make any distinction between what is really good and what is merely pleasant."

Thus saying, the Demon began to shower arrows after arrows on the Devi. The Devi, too, cut them to pieces with her own arrows before they reached her.

She, becoming angry, soon pierced him with arrows. The body of the Demon was then covered with cuts and wounds; blood began to flow from them.

Asiloma then lifted aloft his heavy iron club and ran after Chandika and hurt the lion on his head with anger. Not caring at all this severe stroke of the club inflicted by that powerful Demon, the lion tore asunder his arms with his claws.

Then that dreadful Demon leapt with club in his hand and got up the shoulder of the lion and hit the Devi very hard. The Devi, then, baffled the hit and cut off the Demon's head with Her sharp axe.

The head being thus severed, the Demon was thrown on the ground with great force. Seeing this, a general cry of distress arose among his soldiers. The Devas shouted aloud "Victory to the Devi" and chanted hymns to Her.

The drums of the Devas resounded and the Gandharva began to dance in great joy.

Seeing the two Demons thus lying dead on the battlefield, the lion killed some of the remaining forces by his sheer strength and ate up others, and made the battlefield void of any persons. Some fled away in great distress to Mahisasura.

The fugitives began to cry aloud, "Save us, save us" and said, "O King! Asiloma and Vidalaksha are both slain; and those soldiers that remained were eaten up by the lion."

Thus, they told and plunged the King in an ocean of dire distress. Hearing their words, Mahisa became absent minded through pain and grief and began to think over the matter with great anxiety.

As all his mighty generals were slayed in the war, he had no option but to fight himself.

He, however, was still disillusioned. He thought, "the Devi might not care me, seeing me ugly faced with a pair of horns", and therefore decided to assume a human shape and then go to the battle.

Thus thinking, the powerful King of the Demons quitted the buffalo appearance and assumed a beautiful human shape. He put on beautiful ornaments, arm plates, etc., and wore divine cloths and had garlands on his neck and thus shone like a second Kandarpa, the god of Love.

Then, he went to war on his chariot, which he had snatched from Indra.

CHAPTER 21 END OF MAHISASURA

Story 1: Mahisasura tries to influence by speech

The King Mahisa was angry and also full of dread. He called the charioteer Daruka, "Bring over my chariot quickly."

The charioteer brought the chariot instantly and duly informed the king. That chariot of Indra was drawn by one thousand excellent horses, was bedecked with banners, flags, and ensigns, was furnished with various arms and weapons, and was endowed with good wheels of a white color, and beautiful poles in which the yoke is fixed.

Taking, then, all the arrows and weapons, the Danava in beautiful human shape, mounted on the chariot, attended by his army.

Then, he went to the Devi, elated with power and vanity.

The Devi blew Her conch shell when She saw Mahisasura, the lord of the Danava, come before Her with a handsome appearance, tending to captivate the minds of mistresses and surrounded by many powerful and valiant warriors.

The King of the Demons came up before the Devi and smilingly spoke to Her thus, "O Devi! Whatever person there exists in this world, this wheel of Samsara (the eternal round of births and deaths), be he or she a man or a woman, everyone always hankers after pleasure or happiness. And that pleasure is derived in this world by the combination of persons with each other."

"Union is of various kinds according as it arises out of affection or out of natural consequences. Of these, the union that comes between father, mother and their sons arise out of affection;

and is therefore good. The union between brother and brother is middling, for mutual interests of give and take are there between the two."

"In fact, that union is considered as excellent which leads to happiness of the best sort and that union which leads to lesser happiness is known as mediocre. O Beloved! The constant union of men and women of the same age is considered as par excellence; for it gives happiness of the very best sort."

"Therefore, O Dear! If you establish with me that conjugal relation, you will get, no doubt, all the excellent happiness. Specially I will assume different forms at my mere will. You can enjoy all the Divine jewels and precious things that I have acquired as my queen consort. O Beautiful One! I am your servant, and so I will do anything that leads to your pleasure and happiness."

"I will do, as you order me. I will spend the remaining portion of my life in serving you as your obedient servant. Never will I act contrary to your orders to the risk even of my life. I now throw aside all my weapons before Your feet; O Large eyed! Though I am so powerful, I now acknowledge myself as your servant. Better look at me and grant your mercy."

Story 2: Devi advises Mahisasura

Hearing this, that beautiful Bhagvati laughed loudly and spoke smiling, "I do not desire any other body than the Supreme One! O Demon! I am His Will-power; I therefore create all these worlds. I am His Shivaa (auspicious) Prakriti (Nature); That Universal Soul is seeing Me. It is owing to His proximity that I am appearing as the Eternal Consciousness, manifesting Itself as this Cosmos."

"I do not desire to enjoy the ordinary pleasures. You are very dull and stupid; there is no doubt in this, when you desire sexual union. For women are considered as chains to hold men in bondage. Men bound up by iron chains can obtain freedom at any time, but when they are fastened by women, they can never obtain freedom. Great pain arises from connection with women; you know this; then why are you deluded?"

"Better avoid your enmity with the Devas and roam over the

world anywhere you like. Or, if you desire to live, go to Patala; or fight with Me. Know this for certain that I am stronger than you. See! When words are uttered seven times amongst each other, friendship is established between saints. So, there is friendship now between you and me; I won't take away your life. But if you desire to die, fight gladly. I will, no doubt, kill you."

Even after hearing the Bhagavathi's words, the Danava, deluded by passion, began to speak in beautiful sweet words, "O Beautiful One! Your body and the several parts thereof are very delicate and beautiful. A mere sight of such a lady makes one enchanted. Therefore, I fear very much to strike against your body. O Fair one! If you like, you marry and worship me, or you can return to your desired place whence you have come. You have declared friendship with me; I therefore do not like to strike any weapons on you."

"O beautiful one! What fame shall I earn by killing you! Murdering a woman, a child, and a Brahmin certainly makes the murderer liable to suffer the consequences thereof. I salute before you and speak that a man cannot be happy without the lotus face of a woman; similarly, a woman cannot be happy without a man's lotus face. Where comes off the good combination between these two, then the highest pitch of happiness is conceived and pain arises on the disjunction thereof."

"Who has advised you to renounce enjoyments? O Sweet speaking One! If this be true; then surely, he is your enemy! Leave your stubbornness and marry me; both of us shall then be happy. Visnu shines well with Kamala, Brahma looks splendid with Savitri, Rudra is well associated with Parvati and Indra with Sachi, so I will shine well with you! Why is Cupid not troubling you with his maddening delicate five arrows? Why is he not shooting arrows at you?"

Hearing the words of Mahisasura, the Devi said, "O you fool! Go to the lower worlds or stand up for fight; I will send you and the other Danava unto death and then go away at my pleasure. Know this firmly. O wicked Mahisa! The Devas prayed to Me for your destruction. Therefore, I will not rest until I kill you."

Story 3: Amazing fight between Devi and Mahisa

Hearing these words, the Danava took up his bow and came to the battle, fully stretching the string of his bow up to his ears, and began to shoot sharpened arrows with great force at the Devi. The Devi, too, hurled with anger, arrows tipped with iron and cut off the Asura's arrows to pieces.

The fight between them rose to such a terrible pitch that it caused terror to both the Devas and the Danava, trying hard to be victorious over each other.

In the midst of the terrible encounter, the demon Durdhara came up to fight and made the Devi angry. He shot arrows, all terribly poisonous and sharpened on stones, at Her.

The Bhagvati, then, got very angry and hit him hard with sharp arrows. Durdhara, struck thus, fell down dead on the battlefield like a mountain top.

The demon Trinetra, well skilled in the uses of arrows and weapons, seeing him killed, came up to fight and shot at the Great Goddess with seven arrows. Before these arrows came on Her, she cut them to pieces with Her sharp arrows and by Her trident killed Trinetra.

Trinetra thus killed, Andhaka quickly came in the battlefield and struck violently on the head of the lion with his iron club. The lion killed that powerful Andhaka by striking the demon with his nails and, out of anger, began to eat his flesh.

Mahisasura became greatly astonished at the death of these Asuras and began to shoot pointed arrows, sharpened on stone, at her. The Devi Ambika cut his arrows into two before they came on Her and struck the Demon on his breast by Her club.

That vile Mahisasura, the tormentor of the Devas, fell in a swoon under the stoke of the club but patiently bore it and, at the next moment, came again and struck the lion on his head by his club. The lion, too, by his nails rent that great Asura to pieces.

Mahisasura, then, quitting the man-form took up the lion-form and by his claws cut the Devi's lion and wounded him very much by his nails. On Mahisasura taking up this lion-form, the Devi became very angry and began to shoot arrows after arrows at him all very terrible, sharp and like poisonous snakes.

Then the Asura quitting the lion form assumed the appearance of a male elephant, oozing out juice from his temples and began to hurl the mountain tops by his trunk. Seeing the mountain peaks thus hurled on her, she cut them off to pieces by her sharp arrows and began to laugh.

The lion on the other hand, sprang on the head of the elephant Mahisa and by his claws rent him to pieces. To kill the Devi's lion, then, Mahisa quitted his elephant-form and assumed the appearance of a Sarabha, more powerful and terrible than lion.

The Devi seeing that Sarabha became angry and struck on the head of that Sarabha with Her axe; the Sarabha, too, attacked the Devi. Their fight became horrible.

Mahisasura, then, assumed the appearance of a buffalo and struck the Bhagvati by his horns. That horrible Asura, of hideous appearance, swinging his tail, began to attack the thin bodied Devi.

That violent Asura caught hold of the mountain peaks by his tail and, whirling them round and round, hurled them on the Devi. That vicious soul, then, maddened with his strength, laughed incessantly.

He addressed thus, "O Devi! Be steady in the battlefield. I will send you today unto death, and your youth and beauty too. Really you are deluded in your pretensions that you are very strong. I will kill you first and the hypocrite Devas after who want to vanquish me by standing up a woman in their front."

The Devi said, "O Villain! Do not boast! Keep yourself firm in the fight. Today I will kill you and make the Devas discard their fear. O Wretch! You are a Sinner! You torment the Devas and terrify the Munis. Let me have my drink of sweet decoction of grapes. And then I will slay you undoubtedly."

Saying thus, the Devi, wrathful and eager to kill Mahisasura, took up the golden cup filled with wine and drank again and again.

When the Devi finished her drink of the sweet grape juice, she pursued him with trident in her hands, to the great joy of gladdening all the Devas. The Devas began to rain showers of flowers on the Devi and praised Her and shouted victories to Her with Dundubhi (a Divine drum) Jai, Jiva; victory, live.

The Rishis, Siddhas, Gandharva, Pishachas, Uragas, and Kinnaras witnessed the battle from the celestial space and became very much delighted.

On the other hand, Mahisasura, the hypocrite Pundit, began to assume various magic forms and struck the Devi repeatedly.

The Devi Chandika, then, infuriated and with eyes reddened, pierced violently the breast of that vicious Mahisa with Her sharp trident. The Demon, then, struck by this trident, fell senseless on the ground; but got up in the next moment and kicked the Devi forcibly.

That Great Asura, thus kicking the Devi, laughed repeatedly and bellowed so loudly that the Devas were all terrified with that noise. Then the Devi held aloft the brilliant discus of good axle and of thousand spokes. She, then, loudly spoke to the Asura in front, "O Stupid! Look! This Chakra will sever your throat today; wait a moment, I am sending you instantly unto death."

Saying this, the Divine Mother hurled the Chakra. Instantly that weapon severed the Danava's head from his body. The hot streams of blood gushed out from his neck as the violent streams of water get out from mountains, colored red with red sandstones.

The headless body of that Asura moved, to and fro, for a moment and then dropped on the ground. The loud acclamations of "Victory" were sounded to the great joy of the Devas. The very powerful lion began to devour the soldiers that were flying away, as if he was very hungry.

Story 4: End of Mahisa and prayer by Devas

The wicked Mahisasura thus slain, the Demons that remained alive were terrified and fled away, very much frightened, to Patala. The Devas, Risis, human beings and the other saints on this earth were all extremely glad at the death of this wicked Demon.

The Bhagvati Chandika quitted the battlefield and waited in a holy place. Then the Devas came there with a desire to praise and chant hymns to the Devi, the Bestower of their happiness.

Then Indra and all the Devas, who became very glad to see the great Mahisasura slain; began to praise and chant hymns to the World-Mother.

The Devas said, "It is by your Power that Brahma becomes able to create this world, Visnu, to preserve, and Maheswar to destroy during the Pralaya time (the Great Dissolution) of this universe. But when they are bereft of your Power, they are quite unable to do such."

सौम्यानि यानि रुपाणि त्रैलोक्ये विचरन्ति ते ।
यानि चात्यन्तघोराणि तै रक्षास्मांस्तथा भुवम् ॥

"Whatever your gentle forms wander about in the three worlds, and whatever exceedingly terrible form wander, by means of them guard us and the earth!"

खड्गशूलगदादीनि यानि चास्त्रानि तेऽम्बिके ।
करपल्लवसङ्गीनि तैरस्मात्रक्ष सर्वतः ॥

"Your sword and spear and club, and whatever other weapons, O Ambika, best in your pliant hand, with them guard us on every side! "

After praising the Goddess by hymns, the gods paid honour to her with celestial flowers, and with perfumes and unguents. Benignly sweet in countenance, she spoke to all the prostrate gods, "Choose, you all gods! whatever you desire of me, for I will grant it with pleasure, being highly honored by your prayers."

Those heaven-dwellers spoke, "You, O adorable lady, have accomplished all, nothing remains undone, after that Asura Mahisa, our foe has been slain!

संस्मृता संस्मृता त्वं नो हिंसेथाः परमापदः ।
यश्च मर्त्यः स्तवैरिस्त्वां स्तोष्यत्यमलानने ॥

"Yet if you must grant us a boon, O goddess great! Whenever we call you, call you to mind, banish away all our direst calamities!"

"And who ever mortal shall praise you with these hymns, O lady of spotless countenance, to prosper him in wealth and wife and other blessings by means of riches, success and power do you

incline always, O Ambika, who are propitious to us!"
Being thus propitiated by the gods for the good of the world and
on their own behalf, she, Bhadrakali said "Be it so! ".
She then vanished from their sight.
And again she came into existence having the body of Gauri,
just as she did before, in order to slay the wicked Daityas
Shumbha and Nisumbha, and to preserve the worlds, as
benefactress of the gods and humans.

CHAPTER 22
MANIFESTATION
OF KAUSHIKI
AND KALIKA

Story 1 All deities vanquished by Shumbha and Nishumbha
Of yore, the asuras Shumbha and Nisumbha, trusting in their pride and strength, robbed Indra of Swarga, and all Devas of their portions of the yagya. They both usurped likewise the sun's dignity and the moon's dominion, and Kubera's and Yama's and Varuna's dominion.

They both exercised Vayu's authority and Agni's sphere of action, and they themselves dominated the lordships of every other god, and the kingdom of all worldly kings.

Thus, the gods were vanquished, and deprived of their sovereignties.

Then, bereft of their dominion and set at nought by those two great Asuras, all recalled that never-vanquished goddess, who had granted the boon that whenever in calamities, when remembered, at that very moment, she would put an end to all their direst calamities.

Remembering this, the gods went to Himavat, lord among mountains, and there raised their hymn to the goddess.

Story 2 Prayer of the Goddess
The gods prayed,

नमो देव्यै महादेव्यै शिवायै सततं नमः ।
नमः प्रकृत्यै भद्रायै नियताः प्रणताः स्म ताम् ॥

"Reverence to the goddess! To the great goddess! To Shivaa (her who is auspicious), our perpetual reverence! Reverence to Prakriti, to the good! Submissive we fall prostrate before her!"

रौद्रायै नमो नित्यायै गौर्यै धात्र्यै नमो नमः ।
ज्योत्स्नायै चेन्दुरुपिण्यै सुखायै सततं नमः ॥

"Reverence to her who is terrible, to her who is constant! To Gauri, to Dhatri! Reverence, to you, our reverence! And to the light, to her who has the moon's form. To her who is happiness, reverence to her continually!"

कल्याण्यै प्रणतां वृद्ध्यै सिद्ध्यै कुर्मो नमो नमः ।
नैर्ऋत्यै भूभृतां लक्ष्मयै शर्वाण्यै ते नमो नमः ॥

"Falling prostrate, we revere her who is propitious, to provider of Prosperity! To success in work, we pay reverence! Reverence to Nirriti (Laxmi of Asuras), and to the goddess of Good-Fortune! To you, Sarvani, reverence! Our continuous reverence! "

दुर्गायै दुर्गपारायै सारायै सर्वकारिण्यै ।
ख्यात्यै तथैव कृष्णायै धूम्रायै सततं नमः ॥

"To Durga, to her who takes us to the other shore of the stream difficult to be crossed! To her, who is essence of everything, to her who works all things! And to Fame also, to her who attracts all, or is wine-black! To her who is smoke-dark, reverence to you continually! "

अतिसौम्यातिरौद्रायै नतास्तस्यै नमो नमः ।
नमो जगत्प्रतिष्ठायै देव्यै कृत्यै नमो नमः ॥

"We fall prostrate before her who is at once most gentle and most harsh! To her reverence! Reverence to her who is the foundation of the world! To the goddess who is Action personified our reverence, yes reverence!"

या देवी सर्वभूतेषु विष्णुमायेति शब्दिता ।
नमस्तस्यै नमस्तस्यै नमस्तस्यै नमो नमः ॥

"To the goddess who among all creations is called Vishnu's illusive power. Reverence to her, our continuous reverence to her!"

या देवी सर्वभूतेषु चेतनेत्यभिधीयते ।

नमस्तस्यै नमस्तस्यै नमस्तस्यै नमो नमः ॥

"To the goddess who among all created beings, is present as their Consciousness! Reverence to her, yes reverence to her!"

या देवी सर्वभूतेषु बुद्धिरूपेण संस्थिता ।

नमस्तस्यै नमस्तस्यै नमस्तस्यै नमो नमः ॥

"Reverence to her! Reverence, yes reverence to the goddess who among all created beings stands firm 'with the form of Intellect, Reverence to her, yes reverence to her!"

या देवी सर्वभूतेषु निद्रारूपेण संस्थिता ।

नमस्तस्यै नमस्तस्यै नमस्तस्यै नमो नमः ॥

"Reverence to the goddess who among all created beings stands firm, with the form of Sleep, Reverence to her, yes reverence to her!"

या देवी सर्वभूतेषु क्षुधारूपेण संस्थिता ।

नमस्तस्यै नमस्तस्यै नमस्तस्यै नमो नमः ॥

"Reverence to the goddess who among all created beings, is residing in the form of Hunger, Reverence to her, yes reverence to her!"

या देवी सर्वभूतेषु छायारूपेण संस्थिता ।

नमस्तस्यै नमस्तस्यै नमस्तस्यै नमो नमः ॥

"Our reverence to the goddess who among all created beings stands firm with the form of Shadow, Reverence to her, yes reverence to her!"

या देवी सर्वभूतेषु शक्तिरूपेण संस्थिता ।

नमस्तस्यै नमस्तस्यै नमस्तस्यै नमो नमः ॥

"Our reverence to the goddess who among all created beings stands firm with the form of Energy, Reverence to her, yes reverence to her!"

या देवी सर्वभूतेषु तृष्णारूपेण संस्थिता ।

नमस्तस्यै नमस्तस्यै नमस्तस्यै नमो नमः ॥

"Reverence to the goddess who among all created beings stands firm with the form of Thirst, and Desire, Reverence to her, yes reverence to her!"

या देवी सर्वभूतेषु क्षान्तिरूपेण संस्थिता ।

नमस्तस्यै नमस्तस्यै नमस्तस्यै नमो नमः ॥

"Reverence to the goddess who among all created beings stands firm with the form of Patience, Reverence to her, yes reverence to her !"

या देवी सर्वभूतेषु जातिरुपेण संस्थिता ।
नमस्तस्यै नमस्तस्यै नमस्तस्यै नमो नमः ॥

"To the goddess who among all created beings stands firm with the form of Special occupational efficiency, Reverence to her, yes reverence to her!"

या देवी सर्वभूतेषु लज्जारूपेण संस्थिता ।
नमस्तस्यै नमस्तस्यै नमस्तस्यै नमो नमः ॥

"Reverence to the goddess who among all created beings stands firm with the form of Modesty, Reverence to her, yes reverence to her!"

या देवी सर्वभूतेषु शान्तिरुपेण संस्थिता ।
नमस्तस्यै नमस्तस्यै नमस्तस्यै नमो नमः ॥

"Reverence to the goddess who among all created beings stands firm with the form of Peace, reverence to her, yes reverence to her!"

या देवी सर्वभूतेषु श्रद्धारुपेण संस्थिता ।
नमस्तस्यै नमस्तस्यै नमस्तस्यै नमो नमः ॥

"Reverence to the goddess who among all created beings stands firm with the form of Faith, Reverence to her, yes, reverence to her!"

या देवी सर्वभूतेषु कान्तिरुपेण संस्थिता ।
नमस्तस्यै नमस्तस्यै नमस्तस्यै नमो नमः ॥

"Reverence to the goddess who among all created beings stands firm with the form of Loveliness, Reverence to her, yes reverence to her!"

या देवी सर्वभूतेषु लक्ष्मीरुपेण संस्थिता ।
नमस्तस्यै नमस्तस्यै नमस्तस्यै नमो नमः ॥

"Reverence to the goddess who among all created beings stands firm with the form of Good-Fortune, Reverence to her, yes reverence to her!"

या देवी सर्वभूतेषु वृत्तिरुपेण संस्थिता ।
नमस्तस्यै नमस्तस्यै नमस्तस्यै नमो नमः ॥

"To the goddess who among all created beings stands firm with the form of Occupation, Reverence to her, yes reverence to her!"

या देवी सर्वभूतेषु स्मृतिरुपेण संस्थिता ।
नमस्तस्यै नमस्तस्यै नमस्तस्यै नमो नमः ॥

"To the goddess who among all created beings stands firm with the form of Memory, Reverence to her, yes reverence to her ! Reverence to her, reverence, yes reverence !"

या देवी सर्वभूतेषु दयारुपेण संस्थिता ।
नमस्तस्यै नमस्तस्यै नमस्तस्यै नमो नमः ॥

" To the goddess who among all created beings stands firm with the form of Mercy, Reverence to her, yes reverence to her ! Reverence to her, reverence, yes reverence !"

या देवी सर्वभूतेषु तुष्टिरुपेण संस्थिता ।
नमस्तस्यै नमस्तस्यै नमस्तस्यै नमो नमः ॥

" To the goddess who among all created beings stands firm with the form of Contentment, Reverence to her, yes reverence to her ! Reverence to her, reverence, yes reverence ! "

या देवी सर्वभूतेषु मातृरुपेण संस्थिता ।
नमस्तस्यै नमस्तस्यै नमस्तस्यै नमो नमः ॥

" To the goddess who among all created beings stands firm with the form of motherliness! Reverence to her, reverence, yes reverence !"

या देवी सर्वभूतेषु भ्रान्तिरुपेण संस्थिता ।
नमस्तस्यै नमस्तस्यै नमस्तस्यै नमो नमः ॥

" To the goddess who among all created beings stands firm with the form of error, confusion! Reverence to her, yes reverence to her !"

इन्द्रियाणामधिष्ठात्री भूतानां चाखिलेषु या ।
भूतेषु सततं तस्यै व्याप्त्यै देव्यै नमो नमः ॥

" To her who both governs the organs of sense of created beings, and rules governing all created beings perpetually, to her the goddess of Pervasiveness reverence, yes reverence !"

चितिरुपेण या कृत्स्नमेतद् व्याप्य स्थिता जगत् ।
नमस्तस्यै नमस्तस्यै नमस्तस्यै नमो नमः ॥

"To her who exists pervading this entire world with the form of thinking mind, Reverence to her, yes reverence to her ! Reverence to her, reverence, yes reverence ! "

स्तुता सुरैः पूर्वमभीष्टसंश्रयात्तथा सुरेन्द्रेण दिनेषु सेविता ।

करोतु सा नः शुभहेतुरीश्वरी शुभानि भद्राण्यभिहन्तु चापदः ॥
"Praised by the gods continuously because of eagerly-desired protection, and waited upon many days, may she, the goddess, the origin of brightness, accomplish for us bright things, yes good things, and ward off calamities!"
या साम्प्रतं चोद्धतदैत्यतापितैरस्माभिरीशा च सुरैर्नमस्यते ।
या च स्मृता तत्क्षणमेव हन्ति नः सर्वापदो भक्तिविनम्रमूर्तिभिः ॥
"And she, who is both reverenced as queen by us gods, who are tormented now by the arrogant Daityas, And whom we called to mind as we bow our bodies in faith, at this very moment destroy all our calamities !"

Story 3 Devi Kaushiki emerges from Parvati
While the gods were thus engaged in offering hymns and other reverential   acts, Parvati came there to bathe in the water of the Ganges.
She, the beautiful-browed, asked those gods," Whom do you, deities pray with these hymns here? "
In the same moment, springing forth from the treasure-house, the Kosha, of her body, the auspicious goddess spoke," This is for me! This hymn is uttered by the assembled gods to propitiate me, who have been set at nought by the Daitya Shumbha and routed in battle by Nisumbha."
Because Devi Ambika issued forth from the Sheaths, or Koshas of Parvati's body, she was therefore named as Kaushiki in the worlds.
Now after she had issued forth, the other one, Parvati, became black. She is celebrated as Kalika. she fixed her abode on Mount Himavat.

CHAPTER 23 DHUMRA LOCHAN VADHA

Story 1: Ambika seen by Asuras

Thereafter, Chanda and Munda, the two generals serving Shumbha and Nishumbha, saw Ambika displaying her sublime and most captivating form. They were fascinated, and went to Shumbha.

They told him," We have seen an amazing woman, most surpassingly captivating, who dwells here, illuminating Mount Himavat. O great king! Such sublime beauty was never seen by anyone anywhere. Let it be ascertained if she is any goddess, and let her be taken possession of by you, O lord of the Asuras."

"She is, undoubtedly, a gem among women, surpassingly beautiful in body, illuminating the regions of the sky with her luster! O lord of the Daityas, Sir, deign to look at her."

They continued, "Moreover, whatever gems, precious stones, elephants, horses and other valuable things indeed exist in the three worlds, O lord! All those are in your house! Airavata, gem among elephants, has been captured by you from Indra, along with this Parijata tree and also the horse Uchchaihsravas. Here stands the heavenly chariot yoked with swans in your court-yard, the wonderful chariot composed of gems, which belonged to Brahma."

"Here is the Nidhi Mahapadma, captured from the Lord of wealth Kuber. The Ocean gave you a garland made of filaments and of undying lotus flowers. In your house stands Varuna's umbrella, which streams with gold. And here is the choice chariot that belonged to Prajapati formerly. You, O lord, have

carried off Death's power which is named Utkrantida."
"The noose of the Ocean-king is in your brother's possession.
And he has every kind of gem which is produced in the sea.
Agni also gave both of you two garments which are purified by
fire. Thus, O lord of the Daityas, all gems have been captured
by you. Why do you not seize this auspicious lady, this gem
among womankind? "

Shumbha, on hearing this speech from Chanda and Munda, was
enamoured of the beauty of Devi. He, immediately called the
great Asura Sugriva, and asked him to convey his message to the
Goddess.

He said, " Go to the goddess and ask her to come here. Address
her saying all such things according to such words, and politely
conduct the matter so that she may come to me of her own good
pleasure."

Story 2: Talk with the messenger

Sugriva went to where the goddess sat on a very bright spot in
the mountain and spoke gently with mellifluous voice.

The messenger spoke, "O goddess! Shumbha; lord of the Daityas,
is supreme lord, over the three worlds. I am a messenger, sent
by him. I am presenting his words to you. Please hear to what
he has said, whose command is never resisted among all beings
of three worlds, and who has vanquished every foe of the
Daityas."

"After the introduction, he delivered the message of Shumbha
as follows-- 'Mine are all the three worlds, all gods are
obedient to my authority, I consume every portion of the
yagya separately. The choicest gems in the three worlds are
altogether under my power, and are the finest elephants and the
chariot of the Indra, since I have captured them. That gem
among horses, named Uchchaihsrava, was presented to me
and whatever other created things in the shape of gems
existed among the gods, Gandharva and Nagas, have all been
presented to me. O brilliant lady. I esteem you, O goddess, to be
the gem of womankind in the world. So, I invite you, who are
such, approach to me, since I am an enjoyer of gems. Approach

either to me, or to my younger brother Nisumbha of wide-reaching prowess, O lady of quick side-glances, since you art in truth a gem! You shall gain supreme dominion beyond compare by wedding one of us. Understand and consider this offer, and accept it."

When the goddess heard the proposal, she smiled deeply within herself. She, Durga, the adorable and good, who supports this world, then replied, "Truly have you spoken. You have not uttered anything false herein. I know that sovereign of the three worlds is Shumbha, and like him is Nisumbha also ! But how can that promise made by me concerning myself be fulfilled ?"

" Hear and understand about the vow I made formerly by reason of my small understanding at that time,' He who vanquishes me in fight, who forces my pride from me, and who is my match in strength in the world, he shall be my husband.' So, let Shumbha come here, or the great Asura Nisumbha. Let him fight and vanquish me. Why to delay? And, after winning me, let him lightly take my hand in marriage !"

The messenger spoke, "You are very proud! Do not talk such non-sense before me, O goddess! What male in the three worlds may stand front to front with Shumbha and Nisumbha? None can stand face to face with even the other Daityas in battle, O goddess!"

"Please contemplate! How long can you so stand in fight with him, a woman single-handed! With Shumbha and other Daityas, against whom Indra and all the other gods could not stood in battle, how shall you a woman, venture face to face ? So, go near them with your pride intact. Let it not be that you shall go with your dignity shattered being dragged thither by your hair!"

The goddess spoke, "Even if so strong as this is Shumbha, and so exceedingly heroic is Nisumbha, I cannot follow your advice. How can I, since there stands my ill-considered promise of long ago? So, please return, and make known respectfully to the lord of the Asuras all this that I have said to you, and let him do whatever is fitting."

Story 3: The slaying of general Dhumra Lochana.

The messenger, on hearing this speech from the goddess, was filled with indignation. When he reached Shumbha, he narrated it with some additional spice to the Daitya king.

Shumbha, after hearing that report, was full of anger. He urgently called and commanded Dhumra Lochana, one of the army-generals of the Daityas. He ordered, "Ho! Dhumra Lochana! Go fast together with your army to that shrew, and fetch her immediately here by force, who will be surely unnerved when dragged along by her hair. If any man stands up to offer her support, let him be slain, be he a god, a Yaksha or a Gandharva."

Then the Daitya general Dhumra Lochana went forthwith quickly to the goddess, accompanied by a force of sixty thousand Asuras. On seeing her stationed on the snowy mountain, he cried aloud to her there," O lady! Come forward to the presence of Shumbha and Nisumbha! if you will not approach my lord with affection now, I will take you by force to him. It will be very bad for you since you shall be dragged along by your hair! "

The goddess replied, "You are sent by the great king of the Daityas! You are mighty yourself, and accompanied by an army! Now, if you do thus take me by force, then what can I do to you?"

At this reply, the Asura Dhumra Lochana became extremely angry. He rushed towards the goddess as if to capture her.

Then Ambika with a mere roar, sound of 'hum' reduced him to ashes. Then, the enraged army of Asuras attacked Ambika, pouring on a shower both of sharp arrows and of javelins and axes.

The lion that carried the goddess, shaking his mane in anger and uttering a most terrific roar, fell on the army of Asuras. He slaughtered some Asuras with a blow from his fore-paw, and others with his mouth, and others, great Asuras, by striking them with his hind foot.

The lion with his claws tore out the entrails of some, and struck their heads off with a cuff-like blow. He severed arms and heads from other Asuras. Then, shaking his mane, he drank the blood that flowed from the entrails of others.

In a very short moment, all that army was brought to destruction by the high-spirited lion, who was enraged exceedingly.

This was the start of the end of the Asuri army, finally ending the reign of the cruel brothers Shumbha and Nishumbha.

Next chapter narrates the slaying of great demons Chanda and Munda, and the dangerous Raktabija, whose each drop of blood was converting to a demon replicating him.

CHAPTER 24 SLAYING OF THE GREAT ASURA GENERALS

Story 1: Slaying of Chanda and Munda.

When Shumbha heard that Asura Dhumra Lochana was slain by the goddess, and all his army was destroyed by the lion, he became extremely angry. Now, his command escalated from the level of capturing Ambika to if required, killing her.

In this state of rage, with quivering lips, he commanded his two mighty chiefs of Asuras Chanda and Munda. He ordered, " Ho, Chanda! Ho, Munda! Take with you a great number of troops and go there where that goddess resides. Then capture and bring her here speedily, dragging her by her hair or binding her! if you have any ounce of doubt of doing that, then let her be slain outright in fight. When that shrew is defeated or slain and her lion killed, seize her, bind her and bring her quickly! "

Following his command, Chanda and Munda, took with them multitude of Daityas. They led the Daityas, arrayed in the four-fold order of an army, marching with weapons uplifted, to the mountain, where the goddess was seated on her lion.

Soon they reached there, and saw the goddess on a huge golden peak of the majestic mountain. She was slightly smiling, seated upon the lion.

On seeing her, some of them made a strenuous effort to capture her by hand, and others approached her holding their bows bent and their swords drawn.

Thereat Ambika uttered her wrath aloud against those foes. The countenance of Ambika, then grew dark as black ink in her wrath.

Out from the surface of her forehead, which was rugged with frowns, issued suddenly Kali of the terrible countenance, armed with a sword and noose, bearing a many-colored skull-topped staff.

Kali was decorated with a garland of skulls. She was clad in a tiger's skin.

She was very appalling because of her emaciated flesh, exceedingly wide mouth, lolling out her tongue terribly, having deep-sunk reddish eyes, and filling the regions of the sky with her roars.

She jumped and fell upon the great Asuras impetuously, slaughtering them. She devoured that army of the gods' foes there and then. Taking up the elephants with one hand, she flung them into her mouth, together with their rear men and drivers and their warrior-riders and bells.

Flinging likewise demon warriors with their horses, and chariots with their driver into her mouth, she ground them most frightfully with her teeth.

She seized one by the hair, and another by the neck, and kicked another with her foot, and crushed others against her breast. And, she seized with her mouth the weapons and the great arms which those Asuras abandoned, and crunched them up with her teeth in her fury.

She crushed all that host of mighty and high-spirited Asuras. She devoured some and battered others. Some were slain with her sword, some were struck with her skull-topped staff, and other Asuras met their death being wounded with the edge of her teeth.

Seeing all his force of Asuras laid low in battlefield, in a moment, Chanda rushed against her, goddess Kali, who was exceedingly appalling.

Munda, the other great Asura general covered her, the terrible-eyed goddess, with very swift showers of hundreds of arrows and with discuses hurled in thousands.

Those discuses seemed to be penetrating her countenance in multitudes, like as very many solar orbs might penetrate the body of a thunder-cloud.

Thereat Kali, who was roaring incessantly in a very frightful way, started to laugh terribly with excessive fury, showing the gleam of her unsightly reddish white teeth within her dreadful mouth.

The goddess, mounting upon her great lion, rushed at Chanda, and seizing him by his hair, struck of his head with her sword. When Munda saw Chanda laid low, he also rushed at her. Kali felled him also to the ground, stricken with her scimitar in her fury. Then the army, so much as left alive, seeing both Chanda and Munda laid low, seized with panic fled in all directions.

Kali, holding both Chanda's and Munda's head, approached Chandika and said, her voice mingled with passionate loud laughter, "Here I have brought you Chanda and Munda, two great beasts! You yourself shall slay Shumbha and Nisumbha in the battle yagya. "

Thereon, seeing the heads of those two great Asuras Chanda and Munda brought to her, auspicious Chandika spoke to Kali this witty speech, "Because you have seized the heads of both Chanda and Munda and brought them, you shall therefore be famed in the world by the name Chamunda! "

Story 2: Assembling of the armies of Devas and Danava
After both the mighty Daitya Chanda and Munda were slain, along with a huge number of soldiers, the lord of the Asuras was full of wrath, and gave command to array all the Daitya forces.

Shumbha ordered, "Now let the eighty-six Daitya commanders named Udayudha, march forth with all their forces. Let the eighty-four Daitya Commanders named as Kambu march forth surrounded by their own forces. Let the fifty Asura commanders of the families of Kotivirya, who excel in valour, go forth."

"Let the hundred commanders of families of Dhaumra go forth now at my command. Let the Commanders of Asura families of the Kalakas, the Daurhritas, the Maurya, and the Kalakeya, all these Asuras, hastening at my command, march forth ready for battle."

After issuing these commands Shumbha, the lord of the Asuras, who ruled with fear, went forth himself. He was accompanied by many thousands of great soldiers. Chandika, seeing that most terrible army at hand, filled the space between the earth and the sky with the sound of the twanging of her bow-string.

Thereon her lion roared in exceedingly loud voice, and Ambika augmented those roars with the clanging of her bell. Kali, expanding her mouth wide with her terrific roars, had the predominance over all.

On hearing that combined roar which filled the four regions of the sky, the Daitya armies was very enraged, and surrounded the goddess, seating on her lion, and Kali.

At this moment, in order to destroy the gods' foes, and for the well-being of the Devas, there issued forth endowed with excessive vigor and strength the Energies from the bodies of Brahma, Shiva, and Vishnu and of Indra and other gods also.

These goddesses, went to Chandika. They all resembled those particular gods; from whose energy they had manifested. Whatever was the form of each god, and whatever his ornaments and vehicle, in that very appearance his Energy appeared to fight the Asuras.

In the front of a heavenly car drawn by swans advanced Brahma's Energy, bearing a rosary of seeds and an earthen water-pot; she is called Brahmani.

Maheshwari, the Energy of Maheshwar, seated on a bull, grasping a fine trident, and wearing a girdle of large snakes, arrived, adorned with a digit of the moon on her fore-head.

Similarly, Kaumari, the Kumara's Energy, with spear in hand and riding on a choice peacock, advanced in his shape to attack the Daityas. Likewise, Vaishnavi, the Energy of Vishnu, was seated upon Garuda, and advanced with conch, discus, club, bow and scimitar in hand.

The Energy of different incarnations of Vishnu also arrived.

Varahi, the energy of boar Avatar, advanced assuming a hog-like form. Narasimha's Energy assuming a body like Narsimha's arrived there, adorned with a cluster of constellations hurled down by the tossing of his mane.

Likewise, Indra's Energy, with thunder-bolt in hand, seated upon the lord of elephants and having a thousand eyes, arrived, just like him.

Then all those Energies of the gods surrounded Shiva. He said to Chandika, "Let the Asuras be slain forthwith through my good-will."

Thereupon, just like from the Devas, from the Chandika's body also, emanated her Energy. It was the most terrific, exceedingly fierce, and howling like a hundred jackals.

Story 3: Shiva as messenger of peace

She said to Shiva, who was smoke-colored and had matted locks, "Be you, my lord, a messenger to the presence of Shumbha and Nisumbha! Say to them, and to whoever others are assembled there, these words, 'Let Indra obtain the three worlds, let the gods be the enjoyers of the oblations of yagya. You all go to Patala if you wish to live. But if through pride in your strength, you are longing for battle, come you on then! let my jackals be glutted with your flesh.' "

Because the goddess appointed Shiva himself to be her Doot, or ambassador, she has hence attained fame as Shivadooti in this world.

Story 4: The war

Those great Asuras, however, on hearing the goddess' speech fully announced by Shiva to them, were filled with indignation and went where Katyayani stood.

Then, the arrogant and indignant foes of the world attacked from all sides. They poured on the goddess showers of arrows, javelins and spears. She gracefully, very swiftly, clove those arrows, darts, discuses and axes, which were hurled, with large arrows shot from her resounding bow.

And in front of her stalked Kali then, tearing the foes asunder with the onset of her darts and crushing them with her skull topped staff. She was supported by other mother energies. Brahmani caused the foes to lose their strength and courage by casting water on them from her earthen pot, and weakened their vigour, in whichever way she ran.

Maheshwari slew Daityas with her trident, and Vaishnavi with her discus. Kaumari, very wrathful, slew them with her javelin. Along with them, Indrani was hurling thunder-bolt on Daityas and Danavas, tearing them to pieces. So, the Danavas fell on the earth in hundreds, pouring out streams of blood.

They were further shattered by the Varahi with blows from her snout, and wounded in their breasts by the points of her tusks, and torn by her discus. Narsimhi roamed about in the battle, filing the intermediate region of the sky with her roaring, tearing and devouring other great Asuras.

Asuras, demoralized by Shivadooti with her violent loud laughs, fell down on the earth. She, then devoured those fallen ones. Seeing the enraged band of Mothers crushing the great Asuras thus by various means, the troops of the asuras perished.

Story 5: The slaying of Raktabija

Raktabija, a great Asura, seeing the Daityas, hard-pressed, and intent on fleeing, strode forward to fight in wrath. He had a very special boon.

Whenever from his body, there fell to the ground a drop of blood, at that moment starts up from the earth another Asura of his stature.

He, with club in hand, fought with Indrani, who then struck Raktabija with her thunder-bolt, resulting in immediate flow of blood from his wound.

Thereupon stood up together fresh combatants, like him in body, like him in valour, like him in courage. As many blood-drops fell from his body, so many men equal to him came into being.

And those men also who sprang from his blood fought there with the Energies of deities, the mothers in a dreadful combat, with their very sharp weapons. And again, when Raktabija was wounded by the fall of the thunder-bolt of Indrani, his blood poured forth. From all blood-drops as seed, were born men of similar strength by thousands.

And Vaishnavi struck at him with her discus in the battle. The world was filled by the thousands of great Asuras, who were his equals, and who sprang from the blood that flowed from him when cloven by the discus.

Kaumari struck the great Asura Raktabija with her spear, and Varahi also struck him with her sword, and Maheshwari with her trident.

And the Daitya Raktabija, that great Asura, filled full of wrath, struck every one of the mothers in turn with his club. Whatever wounds he received from the spears, darts and other weapons, progenerated Asuras into being in hundreds and thousands, who pervaded the whole world.

The gods fell into the utmost terror. Seeing them dejected, Chandika decided her strategy.

She spoke with haste to Kali, "O Chamunda, stretch out your mouth wide. With this mouth do you quickly take in the drops of blood, that have come into being out of Raktabija at the descent of my weapon on him. Do not allow the drops to fall on earth."

"Roam about in the battle, devouring the great Asuras who sprang from him so shall this Daitya with his blood ebbing away meet destruction. These fierce demons will be devoured by you and at the same time no others will be produced."

Having enjoined Kali thus, the goddess next smote him with her dart. Kali swallowed Raktabija's blood with her mouth. Then he struck Chandika with his club there; and the caused her no pain, even the slightest.

But from his stricken body blood flowed copiously, and from whatever direction it came, Chamunda took it then with her mouth. The great Asuras, who sprang up from the flow of blood in her mouth, Chamunda both devoured them and quaffed his blood.

Every time Raktabija bled with the wound caused by dart, thunder-bolt, arrows, swords and spears, Chamunda drank up his blood.

Stricken with that multitude of weapons, and losing his blood gradually, he fell on the earth's surface. In this way, the great Asura Raktabija became blood-less.

He died, and the gods gained unparalleled joy. The band of Mothers which sprang from their energies broke into a dance, being intoxicated with blood of demons.

Next, we detail the end of both brothers, Shumbha and Nishumbha.

CHAPTER 25 END OF SHUMBHA AND NISHUMBHA

Story 1 The slaying of Nisumbha

After Raktabija was slain and other demons were killed in the fight, both the Asura brothers Shumbha and Nisumbha gave way to unbounded wrath. Pouring out his indignation at beholding his great army being slaughtered, Nisumbha then rushed forward with the best warriors of the Asura army.

He was accompanied by mighty Asuras on all sides. In front of him and behind and on both sides great Asuras, biting their lips and enraged, advanced to slay the goddess.

Shumbha also went forward, mighty in valour, surrounded with other group of mighty Asuras, to slay Chandika in his rage. After engaging in battle with the mothers, both brothers rushed to attack the goddess.

Then occurred a fierce and desperate combat between Ambika and Shumbha and Nisumbha, who both, like two thunder-clouds, rained a most tempestuous shower of arrows on her. Chandika with multitudes of arrows quickly split the arrows shot by them, and smote the two Asura lords on their limbs with her numerous weapons.

Nisumbha, grasping a sharp scimitar and glittering shield struck the lion, the noble beast that bore the goddess, on the head.

When her lion was struck, the goddess quickly cloved

Nishumbha's superb sword with a horse-shoe-shaped arrow, and also his shield on which eight moons were portrayed.

When both his shield and his sword were cloven, the Asura hurled his spear and that his missile also, as it came towards her, she split in two with her discus.

Then Nisumbha, the Danava, puffed up with wrath, seized a dart and hurled it on goddess; and that also, when it came, the goddess shattered with a blow of her fist. Then aiming his club he flung it against Chandika, yet that was shivered to ashes by the trident of the goddess. Nisumbha, then advanced with battle-axe in hand. The goddess struck him with a multitude of arrows and laid him low on the ground.

When Nisumbha fell to the ground, his brother Shumbha, in utmost fury, strode forward to slay Ambika. He, standing in his chariot, appeared to fill the entire sky with his eight arms, which were lifted far on high grasping his superb weapons.

Beholding him approaching, the goddess sounded her conch, and made her bow also give forth from its string a note which was exceedingly hard to endure. Next, she filled all regions with the sound of clanging of her bell, and her lion filled the heaven, the earth and the ten regions of the sky with loud roars. The combined sound caused the vigour of all the Daitya enemies to die away.

Then Kali springing upward struck the heaven and the earth with both her hands; the boom thereof drowned those previous sounds. Shivadooti uttered a loud inauspicious laugh. At those sounds the Asuras trembled, and Shumbha was controlled by utmost rage.

When Ambika cried out, "Stand, O evil souled! stand! ", all the spectators including the gods, and sages called to her, "Be thou victorious!"

Shumbha approaching towards Ambika, fast hurled the spear flaming most terribly on her. The spear, gleaming like a mass of fire, was driven aside by a great fire-brand by the goddess.

The vault between the three worlds reverberated with Shumbha's lion-like roaring, but the dreadful sound of the slaughter among his soldiers surpassed that.

The goddess split swiftly all the arrows shot by Shumbha, and Shumbha did the same to the arrows that she discharged, each with her and his sharp arrows in hundreds and thousands. Enraged Chandika, then smote him with a dart. Wounded therewith he fell in a faint to the ground.

Meanwhile, Nishumbha regained consciousness. He seized his bow again and struck the goddess, and Kali and the lion with numerous arrows. The Danava lord again covered Chandika with a myriad chakra.

The goddess, then enraged, split those discuses and those arrows with her own arrows.

Then Nisumbha seizing his club rushed impetuously at Chandika to slay her outright, with the Daitya army surrounding him. As he was just falling upon her with full force, Chandika swiftly clove his club with her sharp-edged scimitar. Then, he took hold of a dart. Chandika with a dart hurled swiftly pierced Nisumbha, in the heart, as he approached with dart in hand. When he was pierced by the dart, out of his heart issued another man of great strength and great valour, exclaiming, "Stand! Stand! "

When he stepped forth, the goddess laughing aloud then struck off his head with her scimitar, thereupon he fell to the ground.

The lion then devoured those Asuras whose necks he had crushed with his savage teeth, and Kali and Shivadooti devoured the others. Several other Asuras perished, being pierced through by the spear held by Kaumari, and others became powerless by the water purified by the spell uttered by Brahmani.

Several others fell, pierced by the trident wielded by Maheshwari; some were pounded to dust on the ground by blows from the snout of Varahi. Similarly, several Danavas were slayed by Vaishnavi; Narsimhi, and Indrani.

Some Asuras perished outright, some perished by reason of the great battle, and others were devoured by Kali, Shivaduti and the lion.

Story 2 All Matrikas merge into Durga

Seeing his brother Nishumbha slain, who was dear to him as his life, and his army being slaughtered by the mother powers, Shumbha was in great wrath.

He spoke thus," O Durga, you are tainted with the arrogance of strength! Bring not your pride here. You, depending on the strength of the other goddesses, do fight in exceeding haughtiness! "

The goddess replied,

एकैवाहं जगत्यत्र द्वितीया का ममापरा ।

पश्यैता दुष्ट मय्येव विशन्त्यो मद्विभूतयः ॥

"Alone verily am I in the world. What other goddess is there besides me? See, O vile one! All these goddesses, who have their divine existence from me, are entering into me indeed."

Then all those goddesses, starting with Brahmani, entered and became absorbed into the goddess' body one by one. Ambika then remained alone indeed.

The goddess spoke, "Whereas I existed with my divine power in many forms here, that has been drawn in by me! See, truly alone I stand now! Be now steadfast in combat!"

Story 3 Slaying of Shumbha

Thereupon, commenced a fierce battle between them both, the goddess and Shumbha. This amazing battle, without stop, was looked on by all the gods and the Asuras. With showers of arrows, with sharp weapons and also with pitiless missiles, both engaged anew in a combat which set all the world in fear and awe.

The lord of the Daityas broke all the heavenly missiles, which Ambika discharged in hundreds, with his weapons that parried them. And the supreme goddess in merest play broke the heavenly missiles that he discharged, with fierce shouts, ejaculations and other sounds.

Then Shumbha covered the goddess with hundreds of arrows, and the goddess enraged thereat split his bow also with her arrows. When his bow was split, the lord of the Daityas took up his spear. The goddess split it, as he held it in his hand, with a discus.

Next the supreme monarch of the Daityas, seizing his scimitar and sun-like shield, on which a hundred moons were portrayed, rushed at the goddess. Just as he was falling upon her, Chandika hastily split both his scimitar and shield with sharp arrows shot from her bow.

Now, Shumbha was with his steeds wounded, with his bow split, and without a charioteer. So, as final assault, the Daitya then grasped his terrible mace, being ready to slay Ambika. As he was falling upon her, she clove his mace with sharp arrows.

Nevertheless, raising his fist, he rushed swiftly at her, and brought his fist down on the goddess' heart. The goddess replied by smoting him on his breast with her palm. Wounded by the blow of her palm the Daitya king fell suddenly on the earth.

But again indeed he rose up, and springing upward he seized the goddess and mounted on high into the sky. There, in the sky also, Chandika, being without any support, fought with him. The Daitya and Chandika then fought at first with each other in the sky in a close combat, which wrought dismay among the Siddhas and sages. After carrying on the close combat for a very long time with him, Ambika lifted him up, and then whirled him around and flung him on the earth.

When flung thus he touched the earth, he raised his fist hastily and rushed, evil of soul as he was, with the wish to kill Chandika.

Seeing him, the lord of all the Daitya folk approaching, the goddess then pierced him in the breast with a dart and felled him down on the earth. Shattered by the point of the goddess' dart he fell lifeless on the ground, shaking the whole earth and its seas, islands and mountains.

The universe became placid, the earth regained perfect well-being, and the sky grew pure. Portent-clouds, which were full of flame before, became tranquil, and the rivers kept within their channels, when he was stricken down there.

All the bands of gods then grew exceedingly joyful in mind,

when he was slain, the Gandharva sang out sweetly, and others of them sounded their instruments, and the bevies of Apsaras danced. Favorable breezes blew, very brilliant glowed the sun, and the tranquil sacred fires blazed freely, and tranquil became the strange sounds that had occurred in the regions of the sky.

The gods, then offered a hymn of praise to the goddess. She granted them the boon that she will always become incarnate, and through her manifestations in different forms, deliver the world whenever it is oppressed by demons, or calamities.

CHAPTER 26 LAKSHMI

Part 1 Introduction

Lakshmi: Lakshmi, who is also spelled Laxmi, along with Parvati and Sarasvati, form the trinity of goddesses called the Tridevi.

Lakshmi in Sanskrit is derived from the root word *lakṣh* (लक्ष्) and *lakṣha* (लक्ष्), meaning 'to perceive, observe, know, understand' and 'goal, aim, objective', respectively. From these roots, Lakshmi means," *perceive* and achieve your goal."

A related term is *lakṣhaṇa*, which means 'sign, target, aim, symbol, attribute, quality, lucky mark, auspicious opportunity'.

She, also known as **Shri** is one of the principal goddesses in Hinduism, revered as the goddess of wealth, fortune, prosperity, beauty, fertility, royal power, and abundance.

Lakshmi has been a central figure in Hindu tradition since times immemorial and remains one of the most widely worshipped goddesses even in current age.

Because of her fondness, and seat of lotus, she gets many names connected with it, the most famous ones being Padma, Padmapriya, Kamala, Padmahasta, Padma Mukhi, Padmakshi, Padmavati, etc.

Because of her relation with Vishnu, she is known as *Narayani* (belonging to Narayana or the wife of Narayana), *Vaishnavi* (worshipper of Vishnu or the power of Vishnu), *Viṣhṇupriya* (who is the beloved of Vishnu)

Almost all the names of Durga, are also her name as a part of the Shakti.

Lakshmi holds a prominent place in the Vishnu-centric sect

of Vaishnavism, where she is not only regarded as the consort of Vishnu, the Supreme Being, but also as his divine energy (*shakti*). She is also the Supreme Goddess in the sect and assists Vishnu to create, protect, and transform the universe.

She is an especially prominent figure in Sri Vaishnavism tradition, in which devotion to Lakshmi is deemed to be crucial to reach Vishnu. Within the goddess-oriented Shaktism, Lakshmi is venerated as the prosperity aspect of the Supreme goddess. The eight prominent manifestations of Lakshmi, the Ashtalakshmi, symbolize the eight sources of wealth. These are as follows:

Adi Lakshmi	The First manifestation of Lakshmi
Dhanya Lakshmi	Granary Wealth
Veera Lakshmi	Wealth of Courage
Gaja Lakshmi	Elephants spraying water, the wealth of fertility, rains, and food.
Santana Lakshmi	Wealth of Continuity, Progeny
Vidya Lakshmi	Wealth of Knowledge and Wisdom
Vijaya Lakshmi	Wealth of Victory
Aishwarya Lakshmi	Wealth of prosperity and fortune

Part 2 : Lakshmi in Vedas and Upanishads

Lakshmi is mentioned once in Rigveda, in which the name is used to mean 'kindred mark, sign of auspicious fortune'.

भद्रैषां **लक्ष्मी**र्निहिताधि वाचि

bhadraiṣāṁ lakṣmīrnihitādhi vāci

—Rig Veda, x.71.2

"an auspicious fortune is attached to their words"

In Atharva Veda, Lakshmi evolves into a complex concept with plural manifestations. Book 7, Chapter 115 of Atharva Veda describes the plurality, asserting that a hundred Lakshmi are born with the body of a mortal at birth, some good, *Punya* ('virtuous') and auspicious, while others bad, *paapi* ('evil') and unfortunate. Obviously, here the word symbolizes targets, attributes of a mortal.

The good are welcomed, while the bad are urged to leave.

The concept and spirit of Lakshmi and her association with fortune and the good is significant enough that Atharva Veda mentions it in multiple books: for example, in Book 12, Chapter 5 as *Punya Lakshmi*. In some chapters of Atharva Veda, Lakshmi connotes the good, an auspicious sign, good luck, good fortune, prosperity, success, and happiness.

Shakta Upanishads are dedicated to the Tridevi of goddesses— Lakshmi, Saraswati and Parvati.

 Saubhagyalakshmi Upanishad describes the qualities, characteristics, and powers of Lakshmi. In the second part of the Upanishad, the emphasis shifts to the use of yoga and transcendence from material craving to achieve spiritual knowledge and self-realization, the true wealth. Saubhagya-Lakshmi Upanishad synonymously uses Shri to describe Lakshmi.

Part 3 Shri in Shatpatha Brahmana

The hymns of Shatpatha Brahmana describe Shri as a goddess born with and personifying a diverse range of talents and powers.

In Book 9 of Shatpatha Brahmana, Shri emerges from Prajapati, after his intense meditation on the creation of life and nature of the universe.

Shri is described as a resplendent and trembling woman at her birth with immense energy and powers. The gods are bewitched, desire her, and immediately become covetous of her.

The gods approach Prajapati and request permission to kill her and then take her powers, talents, and gifts. Prajapati refuses, tells the gods that men should not kill women and that they can seek her gifts without violence.

The gods then approach Lakshmi. Agni gets food, Soma gets kingly authority, Varuna gets imperial authority, Mitra acquires martial energy, Indra gets force, Brihaspati gets priestly authority, Savitri acquires dominion, Pushan gets splendor, Saraswati takes nourishment and Tvashtra gets forms.

Part 4 As per Puranas and Epics

Lakshmi features prominently in Puranas and Epics including Mahabharata and Ramayana. In Garuda Purana, Linga Purana and Padma Purana, Lakshmi is said to have been born as the daughter of the divine sage Bhrigu and his wife Khyati and was named *Bhargavi*.

According to Vishnu Purana, the universe was created when the devas and asuras churned the cosmic Kshira Sagara.

(gods) and *asuras* (demons) were both mortal at one time in Hinduism. Amrita, the divine nectar that grants immortality, could only be obtained by churning Kshira Sagara ('Ocean of Milk'). The devas and asuras both sought immortality and decided to churn the Kshira Sagara with Mount Mandara. The Samudra Manthana commenced with the devas on one side and the asuras on the other. Vishnu incarnated as Kurma, the tortoise, and a mountain was placed on the tortoise as a churning pole. Vasuki, the great venom-spewing serpent-god, was wrapped around the mountain and used to churn the ocean. A host of divine celestial objects came up during the churning.

Along with them emerged the goddess, Lakshmi. In some versions, she is said to be the daughter of the sea god since she emerged from the sea.

Lakshmi came out of the ocean, bearing a lotus, along with the divine cow Kamadhenu, Varuni, the Parijat tree, the Apsaras, Chandrama, Dhanvantari with Amrita ('nectar of immortality'). When she appeared, she had a choice to go to the Devas or the Asuras.

She chose the Devas' side and among thirty deities, she chose to be with Vishnu. Thereafter, in all three worlds, the lotus-bearing goddess was celebrated.

Vishnu Purana, in particular, dedicates many sections to her and also refers to her as Shri.

Shri, loyal to Vishnu, is the mother of the world. Vishnu is the meaning; Shri is the speech. She is the conduct, he the behavior. Vishnu is knowledge, she the insight. He is dharma, she the virtuous action. She is the earth, the earth's upholder. She is contentment, he the satisfaction. She wishes, he is the desire. Sri is the sky, Vishnu the Self of everything. He is the Sun, she the light of the Sun. He is the ocean; she is the shore.

Part 5 Lakshmi in other countries

Lakshmi is a goddess in Buddhism and Jainism as well. In Buddhism, Lakshmi has been viewed as a goddess of abundance and fortune, and is represented on the oldest surviving stupas and cave temples of Buddhism. In Buddhist sects of Tibet, Nepal, and Southeast Asia, Vasudhara mirrors the characteristics and attributes of the Hindu Goddess, with minor iconographic differences.

In Chinese Buddhism, Lakshmi is referred to as Jíxiáng Tiānnǔ ("Auspicious goddess") and is the goddess of fortune and prosperity. In Japanese Buddhism, Lakshmi is known as Kishijoten ('Auspicious Heavens') and is also the goddess of fortune and prosperity.

Lakshmi is closely linked to Dewi Sri, who is worshipped in Bali as the goddess of fertility and agriculture.

Part 6 Radha and Lakshmi as per Devi Bhagavat Purana

Of old, in the beginning of the cosmic creation, from the left side of Krisna, the Supreme Spirit, appeared in the Rasa mandala (the Figure Dance) a Devi. She looked exceedingly handsome, of spacious hips, of thin waist, and with high breast, looking twelve years old, of steady youth, of a color of white Champaka flower and very lovely.

The beauty of Her face throws under shade millions and millions of autumnal full moons. Before Her wide expanded eyes, the midday lotus of the autumnal season becomes highly ashamed.

By the Will of God, this Devi suddenly divided Herself into two parts. The two looked equal in every respect; whether in beauty, qualities, age, loveliness, color, body, spirit, dress, ornaments, smile, glance, love, or humanity, they were perfectly equal.

Now she who appeared from the right side is named Radha and she who came from the left side is named Maha Laksmi.

Radha wanted first the two-armed Shri Krisna, who was Higher than the highest; then Maha Laksmi wanted Him.

Krisna, too, divided himself at once into two parts. From His right side came out the two-armed man, and from his left side came out the four-armed Vishnu. The two-armed person first made over to Maha Laksmi the four armed One; then the two-armed Person Himself took Radha.

And for that reason, the Lord of Radha is two-armed and the Lord of Laksmi is four-armed. Radha is pure essence (of the nature of pure Sattva Guna, the illuminating attribute) and surrounded by the Gopa and Gopis.

Laksmi looks on the whole universe with a cooling eye; hence she is named Laksmi and as she is great, she is called Maha Laksmi.

The four-armed Puruṣa, on the other hand, took Laksmi to Vaikuntha.

The two-armed person is Krisna; and the four-armed is Narayana. They are equal in all respects. Maha Laksmi became many by Her Yogic powers (i.e., She remained in full in Vaikuntha and assumed many forms in parts).

Maha Laksmi of Vaikuntha is full, of pure Sattva Guna, and endowed with all sorts of wealth and prosperity. She is the crest of woman-kind as far as loving one's husbands is concerned.

She is the Svarga Laksmi in the Heavens; the Naga Laksmi of the serpents, the Nagas, in the nether regions; the Raja Laksmi of the kings and the Household Laksmi of the householders. She resides in the houses of house-holders as prosperity and the most auspicious of all good things.

She is the luster and beauty of the ornaments, gems, fruits, water, kings, queens, heavenly women, of all the houses, grains, clothing, cleansed places, images, auspicious jars, pearls, jewels, crest of jewels, garlands, diamonds, milk, sandal, beautiful twigs, fresh rain cloud, or of all other colors.

CHAPTER 27
SARASVATI

Story 1: Manifestation of Sarasvati as per Shri Devi Bhgavat purana

Sri Krishna introduced first in this Bharata Varsha, the worship of the Devi Sarasvati, the holder of Vina in Her hands, under whose influence, the minds of illiterate stupid persons become illumined with knowledge.

आदौ सरस्वती पूजा श्री कृष्णनेन विणीर्मिता
यतप्रासादनमुनि श्रेष्ठ मूर्खों भवति पण्डितः

After Lakshmi, Sarasvati also manifested in Rasa Mandala. During Ras-Lila, Devi Sarasvati sprang from the end of the lips of Radha. Because, she was borne in this way from Krishna Priya Radha, she was very amorous, and she desired to marry Krishna out of amorous feelings.

Sri Krishna, the controller of the hearts of all, came to know it instantly and addressed the mother of the people in true words proper to Her and beneficial to Her in the end.

आविर्भूता यथा देवी वक्रतः कृष्णयोषिताः
इयेस कृष्णं कामेन कामुकी कामरुपिणी
स च विज्ञाय तदभावं सर्वज्ञः सर्व मातरम
तामुवाच हितम् सत्यं परिणामे सुखवहम

Sri Krishna said, "O Chaste One! The four-armed Narayana is born from My parts; He is young, of good features and endowed with all qualifications, like Me. He will fulfil your desires. What to speak of His beauty, ten million of the God of love are playing in His body."

"O Beloved! And if you desire to marry and remain with Me, that will not be of any good to you. For Radha is near to Me; She is more powerful than you. If a man be stronger than another, he can rescue one who takes his shelter; but if he be weaker, how can he then, himself weak, protect his dependent from others."

"Though I am the Lord of all, and rule all, yet I cannot control Radha. For She is equal to me in power, in beauty, in qualifications, equal to Me in every respect. Again, it is impossible for Me to quit Radha for She is the presiding Deity of My life. Who can relinquish life?"

"So, O Auspicious One! Go to the abode Vaikuntha; you will get your desires fulfilled there. You will get for your husband the Lord of Vaikuntha and you will live ever in peace and enjoy happiness."

"Though Laksmi is residing there yet like you she is not under the control of lust, anger, greed, delusion and vanity. So, you will live with her in great delight and Hari, the Lord of Vaikuntha, will treat both of you equally."

Story 2 Krishna starts system of Sarasvati Puja

After arranging for Sarasvati, in this manner, to live in Vaikuntha, Shri Krishna declared, "Moreover, I say this in particular that in every universe, on the fifth day of the bright fortnight of the month of Magha, every year, the day when the learning is commenced, a great festival will be held and men, Manus, Devas, and the Munis desirous of liberation, Vasus, Yogis, Nagas, Siddhas, Gandharva, Rakshasas all will perform your worship with devotion in every Kalpa till the time of Maha Pralaya comes."

"All these devotees are required to be Jitendratiya (having their senses under control) and Samyami (concentrating his mind, and with a religious vow). They will invoke you on ajar or on books and then meditate according to what is stated in the Kanva Sakha of Yajurveda and then worship and sing hymns to You."

"Your Kavach (a mystical syllable, which is considered as an armor) should be written on the bark of the Bhurja tree and then with eight kinds of scents mingled with it. It should be placed within a golden nut or ring named Maduli and then hold on the neck or on the right arm."

"The learned should recite your Stotra during your worship".

Thus saying, the Param Brahma Sri Krishna Himself worshipped the Devi Sarasvati. Since then, Brahma, Visnu, Mahesha, Ananta Deva, Dharma, Sanaka and other Munindras, all the Devas, Munis, all the kings and all the human beings are worshipping the Devi Sarasvati! Thus, the worship of the Eternal Devi is made extant in the three worlds.

Story 3: Sarasvati River

Sarasvati continued to live in Vaikuntha close to Narayana, along with Lakshmi and Ganga. One day a quarrel arose with Ganga, and by Her curse, Sarasvati came in parts as a river in Bharata Varsha. She is reckoned in Bharata as a great sanctifying holy and merit-giving river. The good persons serve Her always, residing on Her banks.

She is the Tapasya and the fruit thereof of the ascetics. She is like the burning fire to the sins of the sinners. Those that die in Bharata on the Sarasvati waters with their full consciousness, live forever in Vaikuntha in the council of Hari.

Those that bathe in the Sarasvati waters, after committing sins, become easily freed of them and live for a long, long time in Visnu-Loka. If one bathes even once in the Sarasvati waters, during Chaturmasya (a vow that lasts four months), in full moon time, or on Akshaya Tritiya, or when the day ends, in Vyatipata Yoga, in the time of eclipse or on any other holy day or through any other concomitant cause or even without any faith and out of sheer disregard, one is able to go to Vaikuntha and get the nature of Shri Hari.

Story 4: Method of worship of Devi Sarasvati

All should worship the Devi Sarasvati on the day of commencement of education and every year on the Shukla Panchamî day of the month of Magh (fifth day of the bright fortnight of the month of Magha).

On the day previous to the or the day of worship, the devotee

should control his senses, and concentrate his mind.
After taking his bath, and performing his daily duties, he should install the mud-jar (Ghata) with devotion following the Mantras of the Kanva Sakha or the Tantra, as the case may be. He is to worship first on that Ghata (jar) Ganapati (Ganesha), then meditate on the Devi Sarasvati as per the Dhyan described below. He should invoke Her, and again meditate as described in the Dhyan and then worship with Sodashopachara (sixteen good articles offered in the worship). The offerings as ordained in the Vedas or Tantras, are as follows:

Fresh butter, curd, thickened milk, rice freed from the husk by frying, sweetmeats (Til Laddu) prepared of Til, sugar cane, sugarcane juice, nice Gud (molasses), honey, Swastik, sugar, rice (not broken) out of white Dhan, Chipitak of table rice, white Modak, Havisyanna prepared of boiled rice with clarified butter and salt, Pistaka of barley or wheaten flour, Paramanna with ghee, nectar like sweetmeats, coconut, coconut water, Swastik Pistaka, Swastik and ripe plantain Pistaka, Kaseru (root), Mula, ginger, ripe plantains, excellent Bel fruit, the jujube fruit, and other appropriate white purified fruits of the season, and special fruits and grains peculiar to the place are to be offered in the Pooja.

White flowers of good scent, white sandal paste of good scent, new white clothes, nice conch shell, nice garlands of white flowers, nice white necklaces, and beautiful ornament are also to be offered to the Devi.

Story 5: Sarasvati Dhyan and Mantra

तन्नीबोध महाभाग भ्रमभंजनकारणं
सरस्वती शुक्लवर्णां सस्मिताम सुमनोहराम
कोटिचंद्रप्रभामुष्टपुष्ट श्रीयुक्तविग्रहाम
वह्निशुद्धांशुकाधानां वीणापुस्तकधारिणीम
रत्नसारेंद्र निर्माणनवभूषणभूषिताम
सुपूजितां सुरगणैर्ब्रहमविष्णु शिवादिभीः
बंदे भक्त्या वंदिता च मुनीन्द्र मनु मानवैः
एवं ध्यात्वा च मूलेन सर्वं दत्वा विचक्षण।

I hereby bow down to the Devi Sarasvati, of a white color, of a smiling countenance and exceedingly beautiful, the luster of whose body overpowers that of the ten million of Moons, whose garment is purified by fire, in whose hands there are Vina and books, who is decorated with new excellent ornaments of jewels and pearls and whom Brahma, Visnu, Maheshwar and the other Devas, Munis, Manus and men constantly worship.

Thus, meditating on the Devi, the intelligent persons should offer all the prescribed articles, after pronouncing the Root Mantra.

The eight-lettered Mantra, as mentioned in the Vedas is the root Mantra of Sarasvati. "ऐं क्लीं सरस्वत्यै नमः" (Aim Klîm Sarasvatyai namah). Or the Mantra to which each worshipper is initiated is his Mulmantra (not Mantra).

This Mantra is the Kalpa Vriksha (i. e., the tree which yields all desires).

Narayana, the ocean of mercy, gave in ancient times, this very Mantra to Valmiki in the holy land Bharata Varsa on the banks of the Ganges.

Sage Marich gave this Mantra to Brihaspati on a lunar eclipse; and Brahma gave to Bhrigu in the Badarika Ashrama; next Bhrigu gave this Mantra on the occasion of solar eclipse to Maharshi Shukracharya on the Puskara Tirtha.

Jaratkara gave the Mantra to Astika on the shore of the Ksiroda ocean; Bibhandaka gave this to the intelligent Risyasringa on the Sumeru mountain.

Shiva gave this Mantra to sages Kanada and Gotama, Surya gave to Yajnavalkya and Katyayan, Ananta Deva gave to Panini, to the intelligent Bharadwaj and to Shakatayana in Bali's assembly in the Patala.

If this Bija Mantra "ऐं क्लीं सरस्वत्यै नमः" (Aim Klîm Sarasvatyai namah) be repeated four lakhs of times, the devotee attains success. And when they become Siddhas with this Mantra, they become powerful like Brihaspati.

If one repeats the Sarasvati Mantra, residing on the banks of the Sarasvati, for one month, a great illiterate can become a great poet. There is no doubt in this. Once shaving one's head, if one resides on the banks of the Sarasvati, daily bathes in it, one will have not to meet with the pain of being again born in the womb.

Story 6: Sarasvati Kavach

In past times, the Creator Brahma gave a Kavacha named Vishvajaya to Bhrigu on the Gandhamadana Mountain.

the Kavacha of Sarasvati that is sweet to hear, ordained and worshipped by the Vedas, and the giver of all desired fruits, In the very beginning, the all-pervading Shri Krishna, the Lord of the Rasa circle, mentioned this Kavacha to Brahma in the holy Brindavan forest in the abode Goloka at the time of Rasa in Rasa Mandala.

This is very secret. It is full of holy unheard, wonderful Mantras. Reading this Kavacha and holding it (on one's arm) Brihaspati has become foremost in matters of intelligence; by the force of this Kavacha Shukracharya has got his ascendancy over the Daityas; the foremost Muni Valmiki has become eloquent and skilled in language and has become Kavindra and Swayambhu Manu. Holding this Kavacha he has become honored everywhere.

Kanada, Gotama, Kanva, Panini, Shakatayana, Daksha, and Katyayan all have become great authors by virtue of this Kavacha. Krisna Dwaipayan Veda Vyasa made the classification of the Vedas and composed the eighteen Puranas.

Shatatapa, Samvarta, Vasistha, Parashar and Yajnavalkya had become authors by holding and reading this Sarasvati Kavacha. Risyashringa, Bharadwaj, Astika, Devala, Jaigisavya, and Yayati all were honored everywhere by virtue of holding this Kavacha.

कवचस्यास्य विप्रेन्द्र ऋषिरेव प्रजापतिः
स्वयं छंदश्च बृहतो देवता शारदाम्बिका
सर्वतत्वपरिज्ञानसर्वार्थसाधनेषु च।
कवितासु च सर्वासु विनियोगः प्रकीर्तितः।

The Prajapati Himself is the Risi of this Kavacha; Brihati is its Chhanda; and Sharada Ambika is its presiding Deity. Its application (Viniyoga) is in the acquisition of spiritual knowledge, in the fruition of any desires or necessities, in composing poems or anywhere wheresoever success is required.

श्रीं ह्रीं सरस्वत्यै स्वाहा शिरो मे पातु सर्वतः।
श्री वाग्देवतायै स्वाहा भालं मे सर्वदास्तु।
ॐ ह्रीं सरस्वत्यै स्वाहेति श्रोत्रे पातु निरंतरं।
ॐ श्रीं ह्रीं भगवत्यै सरस्वत्यै स्वाहा नेत्र युग्मम सदावतु।
ऐं ह्रीं वागवादिन्ये स्वाहा नासां मे सर्वदावतु।
ह्रीं विद्याधिष्टातृदेव्यै स्वाहा चोष्टं सदावतु।
ॐ श्रीं ह्रीं ब्राह्मयै स्वाहेति दंतपंक्ति सदावतु।
ऐमित्येकाक्षरो मंत्रम मे कंठम सदावतु।
ॐ श्रीं ह्रीं पातु मे ग्रीवा स्कंधौ मे श्रीं सदावतु।
ॐ ह्रीं विद्याधिष्टातृदेव्यै स्वाहा वक्षः सदावतु।
ॐ ह्रीं विद्याधिस्वरुपा स्वाहा मे पातु नभिकाम।
ॐ ह्रीं क्लीं वाण्यै स्वाहेति मम हस्तौ सदावतु
ॐ सर्ववर्णात्मिकायै पादयुग्मम सदावतु।
ॐ वागधिष्टातृदेव्यै स्वाहा सर्वं सदावतु।

"I pray with good words and Root mantras, Om shrim Hrim, Sarasvati to protect fully my head; to the goddess of Vag, speech to protect my forehead."

"I pray with good words and Root mantras, om Hrim, to the goddess Sarasvati to protect always my ears; with root mantra om Shrim Hrim, to Bhagavati Sarasvati, to protect always my both eyes."

"I pray with good words and Root mantras, aim Hrim to goddess of speech and music to protect fully my nose; with Hrim, to the goddess of knowledge, to protect my lips always."

"I pray with good words and Root mantras, om Shrim Hrim, to Brahmani to protect fully my rows of teeth; to Aim, this single letter mantra to protect my neck."

"I pray with good words and Root mantras, om Shri Hrim, to Shri to protect fully my throat; and my shoulders; and to the goddess of knowledge, with mantra aim Hrim, to protect my chest."

"I pray with good words and Root mantras, aim Hrim, to Devi Vidyadhisvarupi to protect my navel; and to Devi aim Hrim Klim Vani (speech) to secure my hands."

"I pray with good words and Root mantras, keeper of all words to protect my feet; and to Devi Vagadhisththri to protect all my

body."
ॐ सर्वकंठवासिन्यै स्वाहा प्राच्याम सदावतु।
ॐ सर्वजिह्वाग्रवासिन्यै स्वाहाग्निदिशि रक्षतु।
ॐ ऐं ह्रीं क्लीं सरस्वत्यै बुधजन्यै स्वाहा।
सततं मंत्रराजोअयं दक्षिणे माम सदाअवतु।
ऐं ह्रीं श्री त्र्यक्षरो मंत्रो नैऋत्याम सर्वदावतु
ॐ ऐं जिह्वाग्रवासिन्यै स्वाहा मां वरुणे अवतु।
ॐ सर्वाम्बिकायै स्वाहा वायव्यै मां सदावतु।
ॐ ऐं श्रीं क्लीं गद्यवासिन्यै स्वाहा मां उत्तरेवतु।
ऐं सर्वशास्त्रवासिन्यै स्वाहेशान्याम सदावतु।
ॐ ह्रीं सर्वपूजितायै स्वाहा चोर्ध्वम् सदावतु ।
ह्रीं पुस्तकवासिन्यै स्वाहा अधो मां सदावतु ।
ॐ ग्रंथबीजस्वरुपायै स्वाहा माम सर्वतोवतु ।

"I pray with good words and Root mantras, to Devi residing in throats of all to protect always in eastern direction; to Devi residing in tongue-fronts of all to protect always in South-east direction. I pray to Devi Sarasvati, the mother of knowledge to protect always in South direction; and to Devi residing in three letter Mantra aim Hrim Shrim to protect always in South-west direction."

"I pray with good words and Root mantras, to Devi residing in tongue-fronts to protect always in West direction. I pray to the mother of all to protect always in West-north direction."

" I pray to Devi residing in the prose to protect always in North; and to Devi residing in all sciences, to knowledge to protect in north-eastern direction."

"I pray with good words and Root mantras, to Devi worshipped by all to protect always in upper direction; and pray to Devi residing in all books to protect always downwards."

"I pray to Devi who is the root of all scriptures to protect always in every direction."

One should first worship one's spiritual Teacher (Guru Deva) according to due rites and ceremonies with clothing, ornaments, and sandal paste and then fall down prostrate to him. Only then, he should hold this Kavacha. Repeating these activities five lakhs of times, one gets success and becomes a

Siddha.

The holder of this Kavacha becomes intelligent like Brihaspati, eloquent, Kavindra, and the conqueror of the three worlds, no sooner he attains success, or becomes a Siddha in this.

In fact, he can conquer everything by virtue of this Kavacha.

CHAPTER 28
SARASVATI PRAYED
BY YAJNAVALKYA

The Muni Yajnavalkya forgot all the Vedas out of the curse of Guru and with a very sad heart went to the Sun, the great merit-giving God. He practiced austerities for a long time, and then the great Sun became visible to him.

Then, being overpowered by great sorrow, he began to cry repeatedly; and then he sang hymns to Sun God.

Then Bhagavan Surya Deva became pleased and taught him all the Vedas with their Amagas (limbs) and said, "O Child! Now sing hymns to Sarasvati Devi so that you get back your memory." Thus saying, the Sun disappeared.

The Muni Yajnavalkya finished his bath and with his heart full of devotion began to sing hymns to the Vag Devi, the Goddess of Speech.

याज्ञवल्क्य उवाच

कृपाम कुरु जगन्मातर्मामेवम हततेजसम
गुरुशापात स्मृतिभ्रष्टम विद्याहीनम च दुःखितम ।
ज्ञानं देहि स्तुतिम विद्याम शक्तिम शिष्य प्रबोधिनीम्
ग्रंथकर्तृत्व शक्तिम् च सुशिष्यम् सुप्रतिष्ठितम् ।
प्रतिभाम् सत्सभायाम् च विचारक्षमताम् शुभाम्
लुप्तं सर्व दैवयोगान्नवीभूतम् पुनः कुरु ।

Yajnavalkya prayed to the Goddess of speech, "O Mother! Have mercy on me. By Guru's curse, my memory is lost. I am now void of learning and have become powerless, without any memory. O mother, my sorrow knows no bounds."

"Give me knowledge, learning, memory, power to impart knowledge to disciples, power to compose books, and also good disciples endowed with genius and Pratibha (ready wit). So that in the council of good and learned men my intelligence and power of argument and judgment be fully known, and admired."

यथांकुरम भस्मानी च करोति देवता पुनः
ब्रह्मस्वरूपा परमा ज्योतिरुपा सनातनी ।
सर्वविद्याधिदेवी या तस्यै वाण्यै नमो नमः
विसर्गविंदुमात्रासु यदधिष्ठिनमेव च ।

"O Brahm Swarupa! O eternal light! Whatever I lost by my bad luck, let all that come back to my heart and be renewed as if the sprouts come again out of the heaps of ashes."

"O Mother! You are superior to all! You are the presiding Deity of all the branches of learning. So, I bow down again and again to You. O Mother of speech! The letters Anusvara, Visarga and Chandravindu that are affixed, you are those letters."

तदधिष्ठात्री या देवी तस्यै नित्यै नमो नमः
व्याख्यास्वरूपा सा देवी व्याख्याधिष्ठातृरूपिणी ।
यया विना प्रसंख्यावानसंख्यां कर्तुम् न शक्यते
कालसंख्यास्वरूपा या तस्यै देव्यै नमो नमः ।

"Reverence to You! Obeisance to You! O Mother! You are the exposition of the scriptures. You art the presiding Deity of all the expositions and annotations."

"Without your grace, no mathematician can count anything. So, You are the numbers to count time! You are the capacity by which Siddhanta (definite conclusions) are arrived at."

भ्रमसिद्धांतरूपा या तस्यै देव्यै नमो नमः
स्मृतिशक्तिज्ञानशक्तिबुद्धिशक्तिस्वरूपिणी ।
प्रतिभाकल्पनाशक्तिर्या च तस्यै नमो नमः
सनतकुमारो ब्राह्मणं ज्ञानं पप्रच्छ यत्र वै ।

In this way, you surely remove the errors, and wrong conclusions of men. So again, and again obeisance to You."

"O Mother! You are the capacity, memory, knowledge, intelligence, Pratibha, and imagination. So, I bow down again and again to You."

Sanat kumara fell into error and asked Brahma for solution.
बभूव मूकवत्सोऽपि सिद्धांतं कर्तुमक्षमः
तदाजगाम भगवानात्मा श्रीकृष्ण ईश्वरः ।
उवाच स च तां स्तौहि वाणीमिषां प्रजापते
स च तुष्टाव तां ब्रह्मा चाज्ञया परमात्मनः ।
चकार तत्प्रसादेन तदा सिद्धांतमुत्तमं
यदाप्यनंतं पप्रच्छ ज्ञानमेकं वसुंधरा ।

He became unable to solve the difficulties and remained speechless like a dumb person. Then Shri Krisna, the Highest Self arriving there, said, "O Prajapati! Better praise and sing hymns to the Goddess of speech; then your desires will be fulfilled. Then the four-faced Brahma advised by the Lord, praised the Devi Sarasvati; and, by Her grace, arrived at a very nice Siddhanta (conclusion). One day the goddess Earth questioned one doubt of Her to Ananta Deva.

वभूव मूकवत्सोऽपि सिद्धांत कर्तुमक्षमः
तदा तां स च तुष्टाव संत्रस्तः कश्यपाज्ञया ।
ततंचकार सिद्धांतम् निर्मलम् भ्रमभंजनम्
व्यासः पुराणसूत्रम् च पप्रच्छ वाल्मीकिम् यदा ।

Then he being unable to answer, remained silent like a dumb person. At last, He became afraid; and advised by Kashyap, praised you. Then He resolved the doubt and came to a definite conclusion.

Veda Vyasa once went to Valmiki and asked him about some Sutras of the Puranas.

मौनीभूतंच सस्मार तामेव जगदंबिकाम्
तदा चकार सिद्धांतम् तद्द्वरेण मुनीश्वरः ।
संप्राप्य निर्मलम् ज्ञानं भ्रमांधध्वंसदीपकं
पुराणसूत्रम् श्रुत्वा च व्यासः कृष्णकलोद्भव।

when the Muni Valmiki got confounded, he also remembered You, the mother of the world. When by your Grace, the Light flashed within him and his error vanished. Thereby he became able to solve the question. Then Vyasa Deva, born of the parts of Shri Krisna, heard about the Purana Sutras from Valmiki's mouth and came to know about your glory.

तां शिवाम् वेद दध्यौ च शतवर्षं च पुष्करे

तदा त्वत्तो वरं प्राप्य सत्कवीन्द्रो विभूवह ।
तदा वेदविभागम् च पुराणम् च चकार सः
यदा महेंद्रः पप्रच्छ तत्वज्ञानं सदाशिवम् ।

He then went to Puskara Tirtha and became engaged in worshipping you, the Giver of Peace, for one hundred years. Then You certainly became pleased and grant him the boon when he ascended to the rank of the Kavindra (Indra amongst the poets).

He then made the classification of the Vedas and composed the eighteen Puranas.

When Sada Shiva was questioned on some spiritual knowledge by Mahendra,

क्षणं तामेव सचिंत्य तस्मै ज्ञानं ददौ विभुः
पप्रच्छ शब्दशास्त्रं च महेंद्रश्च वृहस्पतिम् ।
दिव्यं वर्षसहस्रम् च स त्वा च पुष्करे
तदा तवत्तो वरं प्राप्य दिव्यवर्षसहस्रकम् ।
उवाच शब्दशास्त्रम् च तदर्थम् च सुरेश्वरम्
अध्यापिताश्च यै शिष्या यैरधीतं मुनिश्वरैः ।

He thought of you for a moment and then he answered. Once Indra asked Brihaspati, the Guru of the Devas, about Shabda Shastra (Scriptures on sound). He became unable to give any answer.

So, he went to Puskara Tirtha and worshipped you for a thousand years according to the Deva Measure and he became afterwards able to give instructions on that scripture for one thousand divine years to Mahendra.

O Sureshvari! Those Munis that give education to their disciples or those that commence their own studies,

ते च तां परिसंचिंत्य प्रवर्तन्ते सुरेश्वरीम्
त्वं संस्तुता पूजिता च मुनीन्द्रैर्मनुमानवैः ।
दैतयेन्द्रैश्च सुरैश्चापि ब्रह्मविष्णुशिवादिभिः
जडीभूतः सहस्रास्य पञ्चवक्त्रश्चतुर्भुजः ।

All remember you before they commence their works respectively.

The Munindra, Manus, men, Lords of Asuras, and Immortals, Brahma, Vishnu and Mahesha all worship you and Sing hymns to you. Vishnu ultimately becomes inert when He goes on praising you by his thousand mouths. Similar is the situation of Maha Deva, when he praises by His five mouths; and so Brahma by His four mouths.

इत्युकत्वा याज्ञवल्क्यश्च भक्तिनम्राात्मकंधर
प्रणनाम निराहारो रुरोद च मुहुर्मुहु ।

"When great personages are unable to praise you, then what to speak of me, who is an ordinary mortal having one mouth only!" Thus saying, the Maharshi Yajnavalkya, who had observed fasting, bowed down to the Devi Sarasvati with great devotion and began to cry incessantly.

ज्योतिरुपा महामाया तेन दृष्टा अत्युवाच तम
सुकविंद्रो भयेत्युक्तवा वैकुंठम् च जगाम ह ।

Then the Mahamaya Sarasvati, of the nature of pure light could not hide herself away. She became visible to him and said "O Child! You be good Kavindra (Indra of the poets)."
Granting him this boon, she went to Vaikuntha.

याज्ञवल्क्यकृतम् वाणीस्तोत्रमेत्ततु यः पठेत
सुकवींद्रो महावाग्मी बृहस्पतिसमो भवेत ।
महामूर्खश्च दुर्बुद्धिरवर्षमेकम् यदा पठेत
स पंडितश्च मेधावी सुकवींद्रों भवेदध्रुवम ।

He becomes a good poet, eloquent, and intelligent like Brihaspati who reads this Stotra of Sarasvati by Yajnavalkya. Even if a great illiterate reads this Sarasvati Stotra for one year, he surely becomes easily a good Pundit, intelligent, and a good poet.

Next, we narrate the greatness of Radha, the goddess protecting blissfulness, and about Gopis and Rasa Mandala.

CHAPTER 29 RADHA AND GOPIS

Story 1: Radha as per Upanishads

Radhika Tapani Upanishad, is an Upanishad belonging to Vajasaneyi Sakha of Shukla Yajurveda (as per some sources it is connected with Atharva Veda).

As per the Upanishad, the noun "Radha" is linked to the verb "Radhayati", which means 'Being supremely merciful, or blissful'.

Thus, Radha is the "Ahladini Shakti", or the "Eternal energy of bliss" linked with, or residing within Shri Krishna.

Radha is the cosmic force, the power that sustains and nourishes the eternal Lila of Krishna.

As per Radhopanishad, "कृष्णेन आराधते इति राधा", or Radha is that who is prayed by Krishna.

Alternatively, Radha is "Aaradhika" of Krishna. Both are devotee of each other.

Radhopanishad also states "राधाकृष्णयोरेकमासनम्।", and "एकं पदम्"; meaning that Radha and Krishna are having same soul, and mind, and their status are similar.

Story 2: Manifestation of Radha and Lakshmi

As per Devi Bhagavat Purana, in the beginning of the cosmic creation, from the left side of Krisna, the Supreme Spirit, appeared in the Rasa mandala (the Figure Dance) a Devi. She looked exceedingly handsome, of spacious hips, of thin waist, and with high breast, looking twelve years old, of steady youth, of a color of white Champaka flower and very lovely.

The beauty of Her face throws under shade millions and

millions of autumnal full moons. Before Her wide expanded eyes, the midday lotus of the autumnal season becomes highly ashamed.

By the Will of God, this Devi suddenly divided Herself into two parts. The two looked equal in every respect; whether in beauty, qualities, age, loveliness, color, body, spirit, dress, ornaments, smile, glance, love, or humanity, they were perfectly equal.

Now she who appeared from the right side is named Radha and she who came from the left side is named Maha Laksmi.

Radha wanted first the two-armed Shri Krisna, who was Higher than the highest; then Maha Laksmi wanted Him.

Krisna, too, meanwhile divided himself at once into two parts. From His right side came out the two-armed man, and from his left side came out the four-armed Vishnu. The two-armed person first made over to Maha Laksmi the four armed One; then the two-armed Person Himself took Radha.

And for that reason, the Lord of Radha is two-armed and the Lord of Laksmi is four-armed. Radha is pure essence (of the nature of pure Sattva Guna, the illuminating attribute) and surrounded by the Gopa and Gopis.

Vishnu took Laksmi to Vaikuntha.

The two-armed person is Krisna with Radha.

Story 3: Radha and Krishna

Brahm Vaivarta Purana states

राधा भजति तं कृष्णं स च तां च परस्परम्।
उभयो: सर्वसाम्यं च सदा सन्तो वदन्ति च॥३८॥

Radha is devoted to Krishna, and similarly he is devoted to her. Both are in every way similar to each other; all sages always speak in this way.

In *Brahma Vaivarta Purana*, Radha (or Radhika), who is inseparable from Krishna, appears as the main goddess. She is mentioned as the personification of the Mula Prakriti, the "Root nature", that original seed from which all material forms evolved.

In the company of the Purusha ("Man", "Spirit", "Universal soul")

Krishna, she is said to inhabit the Goloka, which is a world of cows and cowherds far above the Vishnu's Vaikuntha. In this divine world, Krishna and Radha relate to one another in the way body relates to the soul.

Krishna is Brahm, Param Purusha, who is defined as "Sachchidanand", and Blissfulness is the property controlled by Radha.

Krishna and Radha reside in Goloka. 'Go' does not mean cow only, but also rays, and so signifies different qualities, emotions (Ras), which are divine.

So, this Goloka is not where cows are reared, but which is full of brightness, of all great qualities, and properties.

As per Brahm Vaivarta Purana, Radha comes to earth because of a curse by Sridama, the guard of Krishna.

Radha is the (left) half of Shri Krisna's body; whether in age or in strength or in beauty she is in every way perfectly equal to Shri Krisna. Laksmi and the Lord of Laksmi both worship Radha.

The excellent brilliance of Shri Krisna is overpowered by the beauty of Radha. She is the mother of all the worlds; but no one is Her mother. She is fortunate, respected and proud. She is the Ruling Lady of Shri Krisna's Life and Soul and ever dearer to Him than His Prana (vital breath).

Story 4 Gopis

Gopal and Gopi are those who rear and protect the cows. However, this meaning is true in Vrindavan, where we find human and cow. In the Goloka, the word Gopi refers to the Shakti who protects a particular property, or quality of Brahm. Radha in Goloka is protector of blissfulness, the ultimate property of Brahm.

The word Gopis of Vrindavan in the plural refers to the group of cowherd women who possess devotion toward Krishna. When it is used in the singular ("Gopi"), it generally refers to Radha, who was the Krishna's favorite Gopi.

The prominent *Gopis* are total 108 in numbers. They share the eternal intimate friendship with Radha Krishna. No one can equal or exceed the love they bear for the divine couple. Out of 108 Gopis, the primary eight Gopis are considered as the foremost of Krishna's devotees after goddess Radharani who is considered as the chief of Gopis. Their names are as follows:

Lalita, Vishakha, Champakalata, Chitra, Tungavidya, Indulekha, Rangadevi, and Sudevi.

All the eight primary Gopis are together called as the *Ashtasakhis* (eight friends) of Radha and Krishna.

Story 5: Rasa Lila

Rasa means "nectar", "emotion" or "sweet taste" and Lila meaning "act," "play" or "dance."

Thus, Rasa Lila is more broadly defined as the "Dance, or play of Divine Love."

The Rasa is the playing out of the Vedantic saying of Brahma as "Raso vai Sah." He is of the nature of Rasa, the most sweet and lovely Divine Principle which unites Jiva with Brahm.

Ras Lila or the **Ras dance**, is part of a traditional story of the Gopis' love and devotion for Krishna. It is narrated in the Bhagavata Purana in five chapters 10.29 to 10.33, famous by the name of Rasa Lila Panchadhyaya, or, "the five chapters on the story of the rasa dance".

The bhakti or devotion that the Gopis express in this story is believed to exemplify the highest form of bhakti. In the story, Krishna's flute music attracts the Gopis' attention, making them leave behind their families and homes so that they can enjoy devotion of Krishna.

The Ras Lila takes place one night when Krishna is inspired to play music on his flute. Then, the Gopis of Vrindavana, upon hearing the sound of Krishna's flute, sneak away from their households and families to the forest to dance with Krishna throughout the night, which Krishna supernaturally stretches to the length of one Kalpa, a Hindu unit of time lasting approximately 4.32 billion years.

When they came closer, Krishna playfully disappears and reappears. Krishna talks about love and performs Ras Lila with each of the gopis, assuming numerous forms. The appearance and disappearance of Krishna results in expression of opposite emotions of gaining the love and separation from the love-object.

In the final stage, Gopi's are bewildered with missing of the foot-signs of one favorite Gopi with whom Krishna seemed to elope leaving others. The story ends with the gopis reluctantly going back to their homes after refreshing in a nearby river.

A closer reading of the story leads one to see the Ras Lila as a symbol of "intense devotion to God" and not a "display of worldly lust".

Verse 10.33.40 of the Bhagavata states that, "the person who has heard this story will attain high devotion to the Lord, and then, sobered, he will quickly throw off lust, the disease of the heart."

Gopis are considered as the eternal beloved and manifestations of the internal spiritual potency of Krishna. Among the gopis, Radha is the chief Gopi and is the personification of the bliss potency (*hladini shakti*) of Krishna. She alone manifests the stage of *Maha bhava,* or supreme love for Krishna, and holds a place of particularly high reverence and importance in a number of religious traditions.

The yearning of Gopis for Krishna is like that of soul for Brahm. And when the soul takes complete refuge in Brahm, he takes care of him, and then there is no separate foot-print. Soul is merged in Brahm.

CHAPTER 30 GANGA AND GOPI-RAHASYA

Story 1: Manifestation of Ganga

In ancient times, in the region of Goloka, Ganga assumed the liquid appearance. She was born of the bodies of Radha and Krisna during Ras Lila. So, she is of the nature of both of them and their parts.

Ganga is the presiding deity of water. She is unequalled in Her beauty in this world. She is full of youth and adorned with all ornaments.

Her face was like the autumnal mid-day lotus and sweet smile was always reigning on Her lips; Her form was very beautiful; Her color was as bright as melted gold and She looked brilliant like the Autumnal Moon. Eyes and mind get cool and become pleasant at her beauty and radiance; which were like Radha.

She was of purely Suddha Sattva; Her loins were bulky and hard and She was covered with excellent clothing all over Her body. Her breasts were plump and prominent; they were raised, hard, and nicely round. Her eyes very fascinating, always casting sidelong glances.

Her braids of hair situated a little oblique and the garland of Malati flowers over it made Her look extremely handsome. The sandal paste dot and the vermillion dot were seen on Her forehead. On Her cheeks the leaves of musk were drawn and Her lips were red like Bandhuka flowers and they looked enchanting. Her rows of teeth looked like rows of ripe pomegranates; and the ends of Her cloth not inflammable by fire, worn in front in a knot round the waist.

She sat by the side of Krisna, full of amorous desires, and abashed. She covered Her face with the end of Her cloth and was seeing, with a steadfast gaze the face of the Lord and She was drinking the nectar of His face with great gladness. Her lotus face bloomed and became gladdened at the expectation of a first embrace. She fainted on seeing the Form of Her Lord and a thrill of joy passed all over Her body.

Story 2: Radha comes and sees Ganga

Meanwhile, Radhika came up there. Radha, the governance of Ras Lila, was attended by thirty Kotis of Gopis. She looked brilliant like tens of millions of Moons. Her color was yellow like champak and Her gait was like a maddened elephant. She was adorned with various invaluable ornaments made of jewels. Her pair of clothing were tied round Her waist. They were decked with invaluable jewels and not inflammable by fire (fire-proof). She was going slowly step by step.

The sages began to fan Her with white Chamara. Below the point where the parting of the hairs on the head is done, there was the dot of Sindura on Her forehead. It looked brilliant like a bright lamp flame. On both sides of this Sindura Bindu, the dot of musk and the dot of Sandal-paste were seen.

Seeing Ganga by the side of Shri Krisna, her face and eyes became reddened with anger like a red lotus. When She began to quiver with anger, her braid, with Parijat garland round it began to tremble also. Her lips adorned with beautiful colors, began to quiver also.

She took Her seat angrily on a jewel throne by the side of Shri Krisna. Her attendants took their seats in their allotted positions.

Seeing Radha, Shri Krisna got up at once from His seat with reverence and addressed Her, smiling and began to converse with Her in sweet words. The Gopis, very much afraid and with their heads bent low, began to chant hymns to Her with devotion. Shri Krisna also began to praise Her with Stotra.

At this moment Ganga Devi got up and praised Her with various hymns and asked Her welfare with fear and with humble words.

Ganga, the Governess of the Devas, looked at Her over and over again with a steadfast gaze; but Her eyes and mind were not at all satiated.

Out of fear, her throat, lips and palate were parched up. She took refuge humbly at Shri Krisna's feet. Shri Krisna then, took Ganga Devi on His breast when she became calm and quiet. At this interval Sureshwari Ganga looked at Radha, seated on a throne, lovely and sweet, as if She was burning with Brahma Fire.

Since the beginning of creation, she is the Sole Lady of innumerable Brahmandas and She is Eternal. At the first sight, she looked young as if of twelve years old. Nowhere in any Universe can be seen a lady so beautiful and so powerful. She was auspicious, well-endowed with all auspicious signs, prosperous, and having the good fortune of having a best husband. She was the foremost jewel amongst the ladies and appeared as if all the beauties were concentrated in Her.

Story 3: Radha is angry and rebukes Krishna

At this moment, Radha addressed smilingly to Shri Krisna, the Lord of the world, humbly and in sweet words, "O My Lord! Who is that Lady sitting by your side, looking askance, eager and with a smiling countenance. She is enchanted with your beauteous form and fainting away. Her whole body is excited with rapturous joy. Hiding Her face with cloth She is frequently looking at You."

"You also do look on Her smilingly and with desires. What are all these? Even during My presence in this Goloka, all these bad practices are being rampant."

"It is You that are doing all these bad things often and often! We are female sex; what shall we do? We are naturally, of a very pleasing temper, simple. I bore and forgave all these out of our love. O Licentious One! Take your Beloved and go away quickly from this Goloka. Otherwise, these things will not bid fair to You."

Then, Radha narrates several previous examples of licentiousness of Krishna. From the narration, it is clear that the concerned Gopis are protectors of different Rasas, emotions or powers of Krishna.

Krishna had, on some occasions, given higher importance to other elements, emotions than the element of Bliss. Radha, being the status of bliss, wants Krishna to never be distracted towards such elements.

Story 4: Fling with Viraja

Viraja is specific light, or extreme shining, Tejas. Radha says about fondness towards this quality in Krishna, in a very human way. In Brahm Vaivarta Purana, we read nearness of Krishna to Viraja as the reason of mutual curses by Radha to Sridama, and Sridama to Radha.

Radha complains, "Firstly, one day I saw you, united with Viraja Gopi, in Chandana (Sandal wood) forest. What to do? At the request of the Sakhis, I did forgive you. Then, hearing My footsteps you did fly away."

"Viraja, out of shame, quitted Her body and assumed the form of a river. That is million Yojanas wide and four times as long. Even to this day that Viraja is existing, testifying to Thy Glory (near Puri, Jagannatha)! When I went back to My home, you went to Viraja again and cried aloud "O Viraje! O Viraje!"

Hearing Your cry, Viraja, the Siddha Yogini arose from the waters, out of Her Yogic power, and when She came, you draw her to your side and cast your seed in Her. As a result, the seven oceans have come into existence!

Story 5: Link with Shobha

Next, Radha complained of another Gopi, saying "Secondly, one day I saw you living with the Gopi named Shobha! Hearing My footsteps, you fled away that day also. Out of shame Shobha quitted her body and departed to the sphere of Moon (Chandra Mandal). The cooling effect of the Moon is due to this Shobha."

"When Shobha was thus distressed, you divided her and put some parts to gems and jewels, part to gold, partly to excellent pearls and gems, partly on the face of women, partly to the bodies of Kings, partly to the leaves of trees, partly to flowers, partly to ripe fruits, partly to corns, partly to palaces and temples, partly to purified materials, partly to young and tender shoots and foliage, and partly to milk."

Obviously, Shobha, is the protector of the 'Go' or Rasa(property) of the brilliance. It is not a human cowherd rearer, but another divinity.

Radha is angry because this property has sometime been preferred by Krishna as compared to Bliss.

Story 6: Krishna linked with Prabha

Radha continues, "I saw you united with Prabha Gopi in Brindavan. You again fled away, hearing My footsteps. Out of shame, Prabha quitted Her body and departed to the Solar atmosphere. This Prabha (luster) is fierce luminosity of the Solar atmosphere."

"Out of the pangs of separation, You cried and did divide Prabha. You put some parts in Fire, partly amidst the Yakshas, partly into lions, among men, partly amongst the Devas, partly in Vaishnavas, partly in serpents, partly in Brahmanas, partly in Munis, partly in ascetics, and partly in fortunate and prosperous ladies. You had to weep then after you had thus divided Prabha, for her separation."

Clearly, the Gopi mentioned is protector or rearer of the property of Luster. She is not a human lady.

Story 7: Licentiousness with Shanti, the quality of Peace

Radha continued with other example, "Fourthly I saw you in love union with the Gopi Shanti in Rasa Mandala. On the coming of the spring season, one day You with garlands of flowers on your neck and with your body besmeared with sandal paste and decked with ornaments, were sleeping on a bed of flowers with Shanti Gopi, decked with gems, in a temple made of gems and pearls and illumined by a lamp of jewels. You were chewing the betel, given by your beloved. Hearing sound of my sandals, You fled away."

"Shanti Gopi, too, out of fear and shame quitted Her body and disappeared in You. Therefore, Shanti is reckoned as one of the noblest qualities. Out of the pain of separation, You divided the body of Shanti and distributed partly to forests, partly to Brahma, partly to Me, partly to Shuddha Sattva Laksmi, partly to your Mantra worshippers, partly to My Mantra worshippers, partly to the ascetics, partly to Dharma, and partly to the religious persons."

Radha complained because sometimes Krishna gave more importance to the property of peace than Bliss.

Story 8: Flirtation with Kshama, forgiveness

Next, Radha complains about tryst with other great quality, that of forgiveness.

She says, "Do you remember that one day anointing all over Thy body fully with the sandal paste and good scent and with garlands on your neck, well dressed, decked with jewels, you slept with Kshama (forgiveness) Gopi in ease and happiness, on a nice bedding interspersed with flowers and well scented. You wert so much over-powered by sleep after fresh intercourse that when I went and disturbed, then both of you did not get up from the sweet sleep."

"I took away your yellow robes, the beautiful flute, garlands made of forest flowers, Kaustubha gems, and invaluable earrings of pearls and gems. I gave it back to you at the earnest request of the Sakhis. Your body turned black with sin and dire shame."

"Kshama then quitted Her body out of shame and went down to the earth. Therefore, Kshama turned out to be the repository of best qualities. Out of affection to Her, you divided Her body and distributed them partly to Visnu, partly to the Vaishnavas, partly to Dharma, partly to the religious persons, partly to weak persons, partly to ascetics, partly to the Devas, and partly to the Pundits (literary persons)."

Story 9 Radha rebukes and Ganga hides

Despite being spoken respectfully, the red lotus eyed Radha now began to rebuke Ganga sitting by the side of Shri Krisna with Her head bent low out of shame.

At this time Ganga, who was a Siddha Yogini came to know all the mysteries, and instantly disappeared from the assembly in Her own water form.

The Siddha Yogini Radha came to know also, by Her Yogic power, the secrets of Ganga and became ready to drink the whole water in one sip. Ganga, knowing this intention of Radha, by Her Yogic power, took refuge of Krisna and entered into His feet.

Story 10: Radha searches for Ganga

Then Radha began to look out for Ganga everywhere. First, she searched in Goloka, then Vaikuntha, then Brahma Loka. Then She searched all the Lokas one by one but nowhere did She find Ganga. All the places in Goloka became void of water; all turned out dried mud and all the aquatic animals died and fell to the ground. And Brahma, Visnu, Shiva, Ananta, Dharma, Indra, Moon, Sun, Manus, Munis, Siddhas, ascetics all became very thirsty and their throats became parched.

Story 11: Brahma and others went to Goloka

They then went to Goloka, and bowed down with devotion to Shri Krisna, who was the Lord of all, beyond Prakriti, the Supreme, worthy to be worshipped, the Bestower of boons, the Best, and the Cause of boons; Who is the Lord of Gopas and Gopis; Who is formless, without any desire, unattached, without refuge, attribute less, without any enthusiasm, changeless, and unstained.

They began to hymn Him. All were filled with intense feelings with devotion; tears of love were flowing from their eyes and the bodies of all were filled with ecstasy, the hairs standing in ends. He, who is the Cause of all Causes, was seated in a wonderful throne, built of invaluable gems and jewels. He was being fanned by the Gopas with white chowries, and was seeing and hearing with great delight, and smiling countenance, the dancing and singing of the Gopi's.

He was chewing the scented betel offered by Radha and was residing in her heart, who was the Perfect, all pervading, and the Lord of the Rasa Circle.

Story 12: Brahma Confused in the Ras Circle

The Manus, Munis, and the ascetics all bowed down to Shri Krisna, no sooner they beheld Him. Joy and wonder at once caught hold of their hearts. They then looked at one another and gave over to Brahma the task of communicating their feelings. The four faced Brahma, with Visnu on His right and Vuma Deva on His left, gradually came in front of Shri Krisna.

Wherever He cast His glance in the Rasa Mandala, He saw Shri Krisna, full of the Highest Bliss, of the nature of the Highest Bliss, sitting. All have turned out Krishnas; their seats were all uniform; all were two armed and with flutes in their hands; on every one's neck is the forest garland; peacock's tail was on the top of everyone's crest and Kaustubha jewels were on all their breasts. No one was imperfect; no one was deficient in lordliness.

It was indeed very difficult to make out who was the master and who was the servant. Sometimes He is seen in His Teja form as the Great Light, and there is nothing else; sometimes there is that Clear Divine Form; sometimes He comes Formless; sometimes with form; and again sometimes both with and without form. Sometimes there is no Radha; there is only Krisna; And sometimes again in every seat there is the Yugal Murti Radha and Krisna combined. Sometimes Radha assumes the form of Krisna. So, the Creator Brahma could not make out whether Shri Krisna was a female or a male.

At last, He meditated on Shri Krisna in his heart-lotus and began to chant hymns to Him with devotion and prayed for forgiveness for his misdoings. When Shri Krisna got pleased, the Creator, opening His eyes, saw Shri Krisna on the breast of Shri Radha. There were His attendants on all the sides and the Gopi all around. Seeing this, Brahma, Visnu, and Maheshwar bowed down to Him and sang His praises.

Story13 Brahma prays Radha

Krishna now addressed Brahma and others, "You all have come to me for Ganga. Ganga has taken refuge under My feet out of fear for Radha. Seeing Ganga by My side, Radha wanted to drink Her up, However I will give over Ganga to the hands of you all; but you will have to pray to Radha, so that Ganga becomes fearless of Her."

The lotus born Brahma smiled at Shri Krisna's words and began to sing hymns to Radha, who is fit to be worshipped by all. Brahma said, "O Radhe! Ganga appeared from you and the Lord Shri Krisna. Both of you were transformed before into the liquid forms in the Rasa Mandala, on hearing the music of Sankara. And That Liquid Form is Ganga. So, she is like your daughter and to be loved as such."

"She will be initiated in your Mantra and She will worship you. The four-armed Lord of Vaikuntha will be Her husband. And when She will appear in parts on earth, the Salt Ocean will be Her husband. O Mother! The Ganga that dwells in Goloka, is dwelling everywhere. O Governess of the Devas! You are Her mother; and She is always your Self born daughter."

Story 14: Radha accepts Ganga, who appears now

Hearing thus, the words of Brahma, Radha gave Her assent towards the protection of Ganga.

Then Ganga appeared from the toe-tip of Shri Krisna. The liquid Ganga, then, assumed Her own form and, getting up from water, was received with great honor by the Devas.

Bhagavan Brahma took a little of that Ganges water in His Kamandalu and Bhagavan Mahadeva kept some of it in His own head.

The lotus born Brahma, then, initiated Ganga into the Radha Mantra and gave Her instructions, Radha Stotra (hymn of Radha) according to the Sama Veda, Radha Kavacha (protection mantras), Radha Dhyan (meditation on Radha), method of worship of Radha, and Radha's purascharana.

Ganga worshipped Radha according to those instructions and went to Vaikuntha. Ganga remained as before till then in the region of Goloka, Vaikuntha, Shivalok, Brahma Loka, and in other places, by the command of Shri Krisna.

She is named Visnu Padi, because She appeared from the feet of Visnu.

CHAPTER 31 STORIES OF THREE RIVERS

Story 1 Sarasvati becoming very angry

Laksmi, Sarasvati and Ganga, the three wives of Hari and all equally loved, remain always close to Hari. One day Ganga cast side-long glances frequently towards Narayana and was eagerly looking at Him, with smile on Her lips. Seeing this, the Lord Narayana, startled and looked at Ganga and smiled also. Laksmi saw that, but she did not take any offence.

But Sarasvati became very angry. Padma (Laksmi) who was of Sattva Guna, began to console in various ways the wrathful Sarasvati; but she could not be appeased by any means. Rather Her face became red out of anger; she began to tremble out of her feelings (passion), and Her lips quivered.

She spoke to Vishnu, in anger, "The husband that is good, religious, and well qualified looks on his all the wives equally; but it is just the opposite with him who is a cheat. O Gadadhar! You are partial to Ganga; and so is the case with Laksmi. I am the only one that is deprived of your love. I am only unfortunate. What use is there in holding my life? Her life is useless, who is deprived of her husband's love."

Hearing Sarasvati's words and knowing that she had become very angry, Narayana thought for a moment and then went outside, away from the ladies quarter.

Story 2 Sarasvati curses Laxmi, and Ganga and Ganga curses Sarasvati

When Narayana had thus gone away, Sarasvati became fearless and began to abuse Ganga downright out of anger in an abusive language, hard to hear.

She said, "O Shameless One! O Passionate One! What pride do you feel for your husband? Do you like to show that your husband loves you much? I will destroy your pride today. I will see today, it will be seen by others also, what your Hari can do for you?"

Saying thus Sarasvati rose up to catch hold of Ganga by Her hairs violently. Padma intervened to stop this. Sarasvati became very violent and cursed Laksmi, "No doubt you will be turned into a tree and into a river. In as much as seeing this undue behaviour of Ganga, you do not step forward to speak anything in this assembly, as if you are a tree or a river."

Padma did not become at all angry, even when she heard of the above curse. She became sorry and, holding the hands of Sarasvati, remained silent.

Then Ganga became very angry. Her lips began to quiver frequently. Seeing the mad fiery nature of the red-eyed Sarasvati, she told Laksmi, "O Padme! Leave that wicked foul-mouthed woman. What will she do to me? She presides over speech and therefore likes always to remain with quarrels. She wants to test the strength of us. So, leave Her. Let all know today our strength and prowess."

Thus saying, Ganga became ready to curse Sarasvati and addressing Laksmi, said, "O Dear Padme! As that woman has cursed you to become a river, so I too curse her, that she, too, be turned into a river and she would go to the abode of men, the sinners, to the world and take their heaps of sins."

Hearing this curse of Ganga, Sarasvati gave her curse, "You, too, will have to descend into the world as a river, taking all the sins of the sinners."

Story 3 Vishnu decides the fate as per the curses

While this quarrel was going on, the four-armed omniscient Bhagavan Hari returned there. He was accompanied by four attendants of His, all four armed, and took Sarasvati in His breast.

He began to speak all the previous mysteries. Then they came to know the cause of their quarrels and why they cursed one another and all became very sorry.

Bhagavan Hari told them one by one. He told Lakshmi, "O Laksmi! Let you be born in parts, without being born in any womb, in the world as the daughter in the house of the King Dharmadhvaja. You will have to take the form of a tree there, out of this evil turn of fate."

"There Shankhachuda, the Indra of the Asuras, born of my parts will marry you. After that you will come back here and be my wife as now. There is no doubt in this. You will be named Tulasi, the purifier of the three worlds, in Bharata. O Beautiful One! Now go there quickly and be a river in your parts under the name Padmavati."

He told Ganga, "O Gange! You will also have to take incarnation in Bharata as a river, purifying all the worlds, to destroy the sins of the inhabitants of Bharata. Bhagiratha will take you there after much entreating and worshipping you; and you will be famous by the name Bhagirathi, the most sanctifying river in the world. There, the Ocean born of my parts, and the King Shantanu also born of my parts will be your husbands."

Finally, he addressed Saraswati, "O Bharati! Let you go also and incarnate in part in Bharata under the curse of Ganga. O Good-natured One! Now go in full part to Brahma and become His wife."

Addressing all, he said, "Let Ganga go also in Her fullness to Shiva. Let Padma remain with Me. Padma is of a peaceful nature, void of anger, devoted to Me and of a Satvik nature. Chaste, good-natured, fortunate, and religious woman like Padma is very rare. Those women that are born of the parts of Padma are all very religious and devoted to their husbands. They are peaceful and good-natured and worshipped in every universe."

"It is forbidden, nay, opposed to the Vedas, to keep three wives, three servants, three friends of different natures, at one place. They never conduce to any welfare. They are the fruitful sources of all jealousies and quarrels."

"Never it is for the least good that many co-wives remain at one place. O Gange! Go to Shiva. O Sarasvati! Go to Brahma. Let the good-natured Kamala, residing on the lotus remain with Me. He gets in this world happiness and Dharma and in the next Mukti whose wife is chaste and obedient. He whose wife is foul-natured, is rendered impure unhappy and dead whilst he is living."

Story 4 All three cried and asked for forgiveness

Laksmi, Ganga and Sarasvati wept bitterly, embracing one another. All of them then looked to Vishnu, and gave vent to their feelings one by one with tears in their eyes, and with their hearts throbbing with fears and sorrows.

Sarasvati said, "O Lord! What is now, the way out of this curse, so severe and paining? How long can helpless women live, separated from their husbands? O Lord! I certainly say that I will sacrifice my body when I go to Bharata, by taking recourse to yoga."

Ganga said, "O Lord of the Universe! Why have I been abandoned by You. What fault have I committed? I will quit my body. And You will have to partake of the sin due to the killing of an innocent woman."

Padma said, "O Lord! You are of the nature of Sattva Guna in fullness. Then, how You have become angry! Be pleased now with Sarasvati and Ganga. Forgiveness is the best quality of a good husband."

"I am ready just now to go to Bharata when Sarasvati has cursed me. But tell me, how long I will have to stay there, before I am able to see again your lotus-feet? How long shall I have to remain in my part, the daughter of Dharmadhvaja? How long shall I have to assume the form of Tulasi tree, the abode of yours."

"O Ocean of mercy! Say, when will You deliver me? And if Ganga has to go to Bharata, by the curse of Bharati, when shall She be freed of the curse and be back? Again if Sarasvati have to go to Bharata out of Ganga's curse, when will that period of curse expire? Now, be pleased to cancel your order for them to go to Brahma and Shiva respectively."

Thus, speaking to Jagannatha, the Devi Kamala bowed down at

His feet and embracing them by Her own hairs of the bead, cried incessantly.

Story 7 Vishnu consoles them

Now Hari, always eager to grant favors to the devotees, smiled and with a gracious heart took up Padma on His breast and said, "O Sureshwari! I will keep my own word, also I will act according as you like. Hear! How the two ends can be made to meet. Let Sarasvati go in her one part to have the form of a river and in her one-half part to Brahma and remain with me in Vaikuntha in Her full parts."

"Ganga will have to go in one part to Bharata - to purify the three worlds as she will be urged eagerly to do so by Bhagiratha. And She will remain in her one part in the matted hair of Chandra Shekhar (the Mahadeva with Moon on his forehead), obtained with a great difficulty, and so will remain there purer than her natural pure state. And let her remain with me in full parts."

"O Padme! One of your part will go to Bharata and be the Padmavati River and you will be the Tulasi tree. After the expiry of five thousand years of Kali Yuga, your curse will expire. Again, you all will come to My abode."

"O Padme! Calamities are the causes of the happiness of the embodied beings. Without dangers no one can understand the true nature of happiness. The saint worshippers of My mantra who will perform their ablutions in your water will free you all of your curse by touch and sight."

Story 8 The impact of curses

Then Ganga and others all went to obey the order of Shri Hari, who went to His own abode.

A part of Sarasvati descended in this Bharata Punya Bhumi (land of merits), owing to the curse of Ganga, while She remained in full in Visnu's region, the abode of Vaikuntha. She is named Bharati, on account of Her coming to Bharata; she is called Brahmi because she is dear to Brahma; and She is called Vani as She presides over Speech.

Hari is seen everywhere, in tanks, in wells, in running streams (i.e., in Saras). Because He resides in Saras, therefore He is called

Sarasvan. Vani is the Shakti of that Sarasvan. Therefore, she is denominated Sarasvati. The river Sarasvati is a very sacred Tirtha. She is the burning fire to the fuel of sins, of sinners.

Through the curse of Sarasvati, the Devi Ganga also assumed the form of a river in part. She was brought down to this earth at the request of Bhagirath. Hence, she is called Bhagirathi. While Ganga was rushing down to the earth, Shiva capable to bear the great rush of Her, held Her on His head at the request of the Mother Earth.

Laksmi also, through the curse of Sarasvati came in part in Bharata as the river Padmavati. But She remained in full with Hari. Laksmi appeared also in Her other part as the well-known daughter Tulasi of the king Dharmadhvaja in India. Last of all, through Bharati's curse and by the command of Shri Hari, she turned into the Tulasi tree, purifying the whole world.

Story 9 End of curses

Remaining for five thousand years of Kali, all them will quit their river appearances and go back to Hari. By the command of Shri Hari, all the Tirthas save Kasi and Vrindavan will go along with them to Vaikuntha. Next at the expiry of the ten thousand years of Kali, Saligrama Shila (the stone piece worshipped as Narayana) Shiva, and Shiva Shakti and Purushottam Jagannatha will leave the soil of Bharata and go to their respective places, (i.e. the Mahatmya of those will be extinct from Bharata).

CHAPTER 32 SAVITRI AND SATYAVAN

Story 1 Ashva Pati learns prayer of Savitri

Savitri was first worshipped by Brahma. Next the Vedas worshipped her. Subsequently the learned men worshipped her. Next the King Ashva Pati worshipped Her in India. Next people of all the four Varnas worshipped Her.

The King Ashva Pati reigned in Bhadradesha, rendering his enemies powerless and making his friends painless. He had a very religious queen, whose name was Malati; She was like a second Laksmi.

She was barren; and desirous of an issue, She under the instruction of Vasistha, duly worshipped Savitri with devotion. But She did not receive any vision nor any command even after prolonged worship. Therefore, she returned home with a grievous heart.

Seeing her sorry, the king consoled her with good words and himself accompanied her to Puskara with a view to perform Tapas to Savitri with devotion. Being self-controlled, they performed Tapasya for one hundred years. Still, he could not see Savitri, but voice came to him. An incorporeal, celestial voice reached his ears, "Perform Japa (repeat) ten lakhs of Gayatri Mantram."

At this moment Parashar came up there. The king bowed down to him, and asked the process of Japa.

The Muni said, "O King! One Japa of Gayatri, destroys the days sins. Ten Japas of Gayatri destroy day and night's sins. One hundred Gayatri Japas destroy one month's sins. One thousand Japas destroy one year's sins."

"One lakh Gayatri Japas destroy the sins of the present birth and ten lakh Gayatri Japas destroy the sins of other births. One hundred lakhs of Japas destroy the sins of all the births. If ten times that (i.e., 1,000 lakhs) be done, then liberation is obtained."

He then explained the method of Japa. He said, "Make the palm of the (right) hand like a snake's hood. The fingers should be all close, without holes, and the ends of the fingers should bend downwards. Then being calm and quiet and with one's face eastward, Japa should be performed."

"One should count from the middle of the ring finger and go on counting right-handed (clockwise) till you come to the bottom of the index finger. This is the rule of counting by the hand."

"The rosary is to be of the seed of white lotus or of the crystals, and should be consecrated and purified. Japa is to be done then in a sacred Tirtha or in a temple. Becoming self-controlled, one should place the rosary on a banyan leaf or on a lotus leaf. He should smear it with cow dung, and wash it, uttering Gayatri Mantra. After this, he should perform one hundred times Gayatri Japa intently in accordance with the rules."

"Otherwise, he should wash it with Pancha Gavya (Milk, Curds, clarified butter, cow urine and Cow dung), and then consecrate it well. Then wash it with the Ganges water and perform best the consecrations."

"Then perform ten lakhs of Japa in due order. Thus, the sins of your three births will be destroyed and then you will see the Devi Savitri."

Parashar Muni, then told him the Dhyana, etc., of the Devi Savitri. Then he informed the King of all the mantras and returned to his own Ashrama.

Story 2 Ashva Pati prays and is blessed

The king, then worshipped accordingly. After having chanted the above hymn to the Goddess Savitri and worshipping Her in accordance with due rites and ceremonies, the king Ashva Pati saw the Devi, effulgent like the luster of thousand suns. All the directions were illumined with the luster of Her body.

Devi Savitri then smilingly told the king, as a mother to her son, "O King! I know your desire. Certainly, I will give what you and your wife long for. Your chaste wife is anxious for a daughter, while you want a son. So, one after another, the desires of both of you will be fulfilled." Thus saying, the Devi disappeared.

Story 3 Savitri marries Satyavan, destined to die within one year

The King also returned to his house. First a daughter was born to him, like a second Laksmi. As she was born after worshipping Savitri, the King kept her name as Savitri.

Savitri grew to become a beautiful woman, brimming with such energy that she was often regarded to be a celestial maiden. No man dared to ask for her hand in marriage. On an auspicious day, after she had offered her respects, her father told her to choose a husband with suitable qualities on her own.

Accompanied by ministers, she embarked on a quest on her golden chariot, visiting a number of hermitages and forests. She finally selected an exiled prince named Satyavan as her husband; the son of a blind king named Dyumatsena of the Shalva kingdom. Dyumatsena had been driven out of his kingdom by a foe and led a life of exile as a forest-dweller with his wife Shaivya and son.

Upon her return to Madra, Savitri found her father seated with the sage Narada. She informed her father that she had chosen Satyavan as her husband.

Narada opined that Savitri had made a bad choice. Although Satyavan was intelligent, righteous, generous, and handsome, he was destined to die one year from that day.

In response to her father's pleas to choose a different husband, Savitri insisted that she had made up her mind. Finally, Narada expressed his agreement with the decision, and Ashva Pati consented to his daughter's choice.

Ashva Pati and Savitri approached Dyumatsena and Satyavan in the forest to propose the marriage, which was joyfully accepted.

Savitri and Satyavan were soon married. The King betrothed her with jewels and ornaments.

Story 4 Savitri does penance till time of death of Satyavan

Immediately after the wedding, Savitri discarded her jewelry and adopted the bark and red garment attire of a hermit, and lived in perfect obedience and respect to her new parents-in-law and husband.

Despite her happiness, she could not stop dwelling on the words of Narada. Three days before the destined death of Satyavan, Savitri started to observe a vow of fasting and stood day and night chanting the Savitri Mantra.

Her father-in-law worried that she had taken on too harsh a regimen, but Savitri replied that she has taken an oath to perform these austerities, to which Dyumatsena offered his support.

The day of her husband's predicted demise, Savitri offered oblations to the fire and obeisance to the Brahmanas, completing her vow.

She joined Satyavan when he went to chop wood. Growing fatigued due to exertion, he conveyed his desire to sleep to his wife, who placed his head on her lap.

Yama, the god of death, personally arrived to collect the soul of Satyavan with his noose. Distressed, Savitri followed Yama as he carried her husband's soul away.

Story 5 Yama asks Savitri to go back

The high souled Yama seeing Savitri following Him, addressed her sweetly, "O Savitri! Where are you going in this mortal coil? If you like to follow after all, then quit this body. The mortal man, with his transient coil of these five elements, is not able to go to My Abode. O Chaste One! The death time of your husband arrived; therefore, Satyavan is going to My Abode to reap the fruits of his Karma."

Seeing Savitri continuing to follow, Yama said, "Every living animal is born by his Karma. He dies again through his lifelong Karma. It is his Karma alone that ordains pleasure, pain, fear, sorrows, etc. By Karma, this embodied soul here becomes Indra;

by Karma he can become a Brahma's son. Jiva, by his Karma, can be in Hari's service and be free from birth and death!"

"By one's own Karma all sorts of Siddhis and immortality can be obtained. By Karma, a being becomes divine, human, or a King, or Shiva or Ganesha! The state of Munindra, Tapasvi, Mlechchha, different Varnas, moving things, stones, Rakshasa, Kinnaras, Kingship, becoming trees, beasts, forest animals, inferior animals, worms, Daityas, Danava, Asuras, all are fashioned and wrought by Karma and Karma alone."

Hearing the words of Yama, the chaste intelligent Savitri, replied with great devotion, "O Dharmaraja! What is Karma? Why and how is its origin? What is the cause of Karma? Who is the embodied soul (bound by Karma)? What is this body? And who is it that does Karma?"

Dharma said, "Karma is of two kinds: good and bad. The Karma that is stated in the Vedas as leading to Dharma is good, and all other actions are bad. The God's service, without any selfish ends (Sankalpa) and without the hope of any fruits thereof, is of such a nature as to root out all the Karmas and gives rise to the highest devotion to God. A man who is such a Bhakta of Brahma becomes liberated, so the Shrutis say. Who then does the Karma and who is it that enjoys? (i.e., no such body). To such a Bhakta to Brahma, there is no birth, death, old age, disease, sorrow nor any fear."

Savitri continued to follow, and asked further, "What is Jnana? What is Buddhi? What is this Prana of this embodied Jiva? What are the Indriyas? And what are their characteristics? And what are the Devatas thereof? Who is it that enjoys and who is it that makes one enjoy? What is this enjoyment (Bhoga)? And what is the means of escape from it? And what is the nature of that State when one escapes from enjoyment? What is the nature of Jivatma? And what of Paramatma? O Deva! Speak all these in detail to me."

Yama was happy to reply such questions from a damsel. He said, "O Chaste One! Bhakti is two-fold. This is stated by all in the Shrutis. The one leads to Nirvana and the other leads to the nature of Hari. The Vaishnavas want the Bhakti to Hari, i.e., the Saguna Bhakti. The other Yogis and the best knowers of Brahma want the Nirguna Bhakti. He who is the Seed of Karma, and the Bestower of the fruits of Karma, who is the Karma Incarnate and the Mula Prakriti, is the Bhagavan. He is the Highest Self. He is the Material Cause of Karma."

"Know this body to be by nature liable to dissolve and die. Earth, air, akasha, water, and fire; these are the threads of the work of creation of Brahma. The Embodied Soul is the Doer of Karma, the Karta. He is the enjoyer; and Aatma (self) is the prompter, the stimulator within to do the Karma and enjoy the fruits thereof. The experiencing of pleasures and pains and the varieties thereof is known as Bhoga. Liberation, Mukti is the escape therefrom."

"The knowledge by which Aatma (sat) and Maya (Asat) are discriminated is called Brahma Vidya. The knowledge is considered as the root discriminator of various objects of enjoyments. By Buddhi is meant the right seeing of things. It is considered as the seed of Gyan. Prana is the strength of the embodied. Mind is the chief, the best, of the senses, it is a part of Ishvara. It impels to all actions. It is invisible, and also obstructs the Gyan. The senses are the several limbs, as it were, of the embodied and the impellers to all actions. They are both enemies and friends."

"The Sun, Vayu, Earth, Brahma and others are their Devatas. The Jiva is the holder, the sustainer of Prana, body, etc. The Paramatma, the Highest Self, is the Best of all, Omnipresent, transcending the Gunas, and beyond Prakriti. He is the Cause of all causes and He is the Brahma Itself. O Chaste One! I have replied, according to the Shastras to all your questions. These are real knowledge. O Child! Now go back to your house at pleasure."

Savitri replied, "Whither shall I go, leaving my Husband and You, the Ocean of Knowledge? Please answer the queries that I now put to Thee. What wombs do the Jiva get in response to which Karmas? What Karmas lead to the Heavens? And what Karmas lead to various hells? Which Karmas lead to Mukti?

And which Karmas give Bhakti? What Karmas make one Yogi and what Karmas inflict diseases? Which Karmas make one's life long? or short? Which Karmas again make one happy? And what Karmas make one miserable? Which Karmas make one deformed in one's limbs, one-eyed, blind, deaf, lame or idiotic?"

Story 6 Savitri gets boons from Yama

Yama replied to all her queries. He was very happy with the wisdom of the young girl. He praised both the content and diction of her words and offered to grant her any boon of her choice, except the life of Satyavan.

Savitri first requested the restoration of her blind father-in-law Dyumatsena's sight and strength, which Yama grants.

As they continued, she secured another boon for Dyumatsena to regain his lost kingdom. Pleased by her insight, Yama granted her a third boon, allowing his father Ashwapati to have a hundred sons to continue his lineage.

Even after receiving these favors, Savitri refused to turn back and continued to walk alongside Yama, discussing morality and righteousness.

Yama, further impressed, granted her a fourth boon: a hundred sons for herself and Satyavan.

At this point, Savitri cleverly argued that the fulfillment of this boon would be meaningless without her husband, as she could only bear sons with him.

Yama, realizing her wisdom and devotion, relented and restored Satyavan's life and blessed both of them with a long life.

With Yama's blessings, Savitri returned to the forest and placed Satyavan's head on her lap. He regained consciousness, confused, but she reassured him.

As Satyavan and Savitri had not returned, Dyumatsena, having regained his sight, searched anxiously for his son. The sages reassured him, predicting Satyavan's survival due to Savitri's virtue. Late at night, the couple arrived at the hermitage, bringing relief to all.

Savitri recounted to all her encounter with Yama and the boons granted—her father-in-law's sight and kingdom, a hundred sons for her father, and the same for herself and Satyavan.

The next morning, messengers announced Dyumatsena's restoration to the throne, as his usurper has been slain. He returned to his kingdom with his family, and in time, Savitri was mother of a hundred sons, securing their lineage.

Story 7 Vat Savitri Puja

In Eastern Indian states including Bihar, Jharkhand, and Odisha, married women observe Vat Savitri Vrata on the Amavasya (new moon) day in the month of Jyestha every year. This is performed for the well-being and long life of their husbands. A treatise entitled *Savitri Brata Katha* in is read out by women while performing the puja.

In Western India, the holy day is observed on the Purnima (full moon) of the month as Vat Purnima.

In India, many girls are named "Savitri".

Similar Vrata is observed in South India also. It is believed that Savitri got her husband back on the first day of the Tamil month Panguni. This day is celebrated as *Karadayan Nonbu* in Tamil Nadu.

On this day, married women and young girls wear yellow robes and pray to Hindu goddesses for long lives for their husbands. Girls start this practice at a very young age; they wear a yellow robe on this day from the time they are a year old so they will find a good husband in future.

In the next chapter, we read about Vedavathi, who took birth as Shadow Sita to destroy Ravana, and again as Draupadi.

CHAPTER 33 STORY OF VEDAVATHI

Story 1 Shiva becomes angry on Surya

The Manu Daksa Savarni was very religious, devoted to Visnu, of wide renown, of a great name, and born with Visnu's parts. Daksa Savarni's son Brahma Savarni was also very religious, devoted to Visnu and of a pure Shuddha Sattva Guna. Brahma Savarni's son, Dharma Savarni was devoted to Visnu and He was the master of his senses.

Dharma Savarni's sons Rudra Savarni was also a man of restraint and very devoted. Rudra Savarni's son was Deva Savarni, devoted to Visnu. Deva Savarni's son was Indra Savarni. He was a great Bhakta of Visnu. His son was Vrisadhvaja.

Vrisadhvaja was highly devoted to Shiva. At his house Shiva Himself remained for three Deva Yugas. So much so that Bhagavan Bhoothnath loved him more than his own son.

Vrisadhvaja became a fanatic Shaiva. He did not recognise Narayana, nor Laksmi nor Sarasvati nor another body. He discarded the worship of all the Devas. He worshipped Shankara only.

Vrisadhvaja put an entire stop to the greatly exciting Laksmi Puja (worship of Maha Laksmi) in the month of Bhadra and Shri Panchami Puja of Sarasvati in the month of Magha. At this the Sun became angry with the King Vrisadhvaja, the discarder of the holy thread

He cursed Him thus, "O King! As you are purely devoted to Shiva and Shiva alone, and as you do not recognise any other Devas, I say within no time, you will be deprived of all your wealth and prosperity."

Shankara, hearing this curse, became very angry and taking His trident, ran after the Sun.

Story 2 Sun takes refuge with Vishnu

The Sun, becoming afraid, accompanied His father Kashyap and took refuge of Brahma. Bhagavan Shankara followed him to the Brahma Loka, with trident in His hands.

Brahma became afraid of Mahadeva and took Sun to the region of Vaikuntha. Out of terror, the throats of Brahma, Kashyap, and Sun became parched and dry and they all went afraid for refuge to Narayana, the Lord of all. They all bowed down to Him and praised Him frequently and finally informed Him of the cause of their coming and why they were so much afraid.

Narayana showed them mercy, and granted them "Abhaya" (no fear).

He said, "Please take rest. Why are you afraid, when I am here! Whoever remembers Me, wherever he may be, involved in danger or fear, I go there with the Sudarshan disc in My hand and save him. O Devas! In the form of Brahma, I am the Creator; and in the form of Mahesha, I am the Destroyer. I am Shiva; I am you; and I am the Surya, composed of the three qualities."

Bhagavan Shankara always hears the words of His Bhaktas; and He is kind to them. He is their Self. Both the Sun and Shiva are dearer to Me than My life. No one is more energetic than Sankara and the Sun. Mahadeva can easily create ten million Suns and ten million Brahmas. There is nothing impossible for him. Having no consciousness of any outer thing, immersed, day and night, in meditating on Me with His whole heart concentrated, He is repeating with devotion My Mantra from His five faces and He always sings My glories.

I am also thinking, day and night, of His welfare. Whoever worships Me in whichever way, I also favour him similarly. Bhagavan Maha Deva is of the nature of Shiva, all auspiciousness. It is because liberation is obtained from Him, He is called Shiva.

Story 3 Vishnu reconciles

While Narayana was thus speaking, the trident holder Mahadeva, with his eyes red like reddened lotuses, mounting on His bull, came up there and getting down from His Bull, humbly bowed down with devotion to the Lord of Laksmi, peaceful and higher than the highest. Narayana was then seated on His throne, decked with jewel ornaments.

When Mahadeva bowed down to Narayana, Brahma also bowed down to Mahadeva. The Sun, too, surprised, bowed down to Mahadeva with devotion. Kashyap, too, bowed and with great bhakti, began to praise Mahadeva.

On the other hand, Shankara praised Narayana and took His seat on the throne. The attendants of Narayana began to fan Mahadeva with white chowries. Then Visnu addressed Him with sweet nectar-like voice and said, "O Maheshwar! What brings you here? Why you are angry?"

Mahadeva said, "O Visnu! The King Vrisadhavaja is my great devotee. He is dearer to Me than My life. The Sun has cursed him and so I am angry. Out of the affection for a son I am ready to kill Surya. O Lord of the world! Now tell me what becomes of My stupid Bhakta who has become devoid of fortune and prosperity by the curse of Surya."

Visnu said, "O Sankara! Twenty-one yugas elapsed within this one-half Ghatika, by the coincidence of Fate (Daiva). Through the unavoidable coincidence of the cruel Fate, Vrisadhvaja died. His son Rathadhvaja, too, died. Rathadhvaja had two noble sons Dharmadhvaja and Kushadhvaja. Both of them are great Vaishnavas; but, through Surya's curse, they have become luckless. Their kingdoms are lost; they have become destitute of all property; prosperity and they are now engaged in worshipping Maha Laksmi."

"Maha Laksmi will be born as daughter to him. Then again, by the grace of Laksmi, Dharmadhvaja and Kushadhvaja will be prosperous and become great Kings. O Shambhu Your worshipper Vrisadhvaja is dead. Therefore, go back to your place. O Brahma, O Sun! O Kashyap! You all also better go to your places

respectively."
Story 4: Birth and Tapasya of Vedavathi
Dharmadhvaja and Kushadhvaja practised severe Tapasya and worshipped Laksmi. They then got separately their desired boons. By the boon of Maha Laksmi, they became again the rulers of the earth.

They acquired great religious merits and they also had their children. Malavati, the chaste wife of Kushadhvaja, delivered one daughter, part incarnation of Kamala.

The daughter, on being born, became full of wisdom. On being born, the baby began to sing clearly the Vedic mantras. The four Vedas reigned incarnate, in their true forms, on her lips. Therefore, she was named Vedavathi by the Pundits.

She bathed soon after her birth and became ready to go to the forest to practise severe tapas. Everyone then, tried earnestly to dissuade her, devoted to Narayana, from the enterprise. But she did not listen to anybody.

She went to Puskara and practiced hard Tapasya for one Manvantara. Yet her body did not get lean a bit; rather she grew more plumpy and fatter. By degrees her youth began to show signs in her body. One day she heard an incorporeal voice from the air above, "O Fair One! In your next birth Shri Hari, adored by Brahma and other gods, will be your husband."

Story 5: Ravana cursed
Hearing this, her joy knew no bounds. She went to the solitary caves in the Gandha Madan Mountain to practise tapas again. When a long time passed away in this Tapasya, one day the irresistible Ravana came there as guest. No sooner Vedavathi saw the guest, then she gave him, out of devotion to the guest, water to wash feet, delicious fruits, and cool water for his drink. The villain accepting the hospitality and sitting there, began to ask, "O Auspicious One! Who are you?"

Seeing the fair smiling lady, with beautiful teeth, her face blooming like the autumnal lotus, of heavy loins, and of full breast, that villain became passionate. He lost entirely all consciousness and became ready to take her with violence.

Seeing this, the chaste Vedavathi, became angry and out of her tapas influence, astounded him and made him insensible to move. He remained motionless like an inanimate body. He could not move his hands nor feet nor could he speak.

That wicked fellow then mentally recited praises to her. And the praise of the Higher Shakti can never go futile. She became pleased and granted him religious merits in the next world. But she also pronounced this curse, "Since you have touched my body out of passion, you will be ruined with your whole family for my sake."

Thus, saying to Ravana, Vedavathi left her body by her yogic power. Then Ravana took her body and delivered it to the Ganges and he then returned to his own home. But Ravana thought over the matter repeatedly and exclaimed, "What wonder have I seen! Oh! What a miracle this lady has wrought!" Ravana thus lamented continuously.

Story 6: Vedavathi as Sita

This Vedavathi, of pure character, took her birth afterwards as Sita, the daughter of Janaka. For the sake of this Sita, Ravana was ruined with his whole family.

By the religious merits of her previous birth, the ascetic lady got Bhagavan Hari Shri Rama Chandra, the Fullest of the Full, for her husband and remained for a long time in great enjoyment with the Lord of the world; a thing very difficult to be attained!

Though she was a Jatismara (one who knows all about her past lives), she did not feel any pain due to her practising severe austerities in her previous birth; for when the pains end in success, the pains are not then felt at all.

Sita, in Her fresh youth enjoyed various pleasures in the company of her husband, handsome, peaceful, humorous and witty, the chief of the Devas, loved by the female sex, well-qualified, and just what she desired.

But the all-powerful Time is irresistible; the truthful Ramachandra, the scion of the Raghu's family, had to keep up the promise made by his father and so he had to go to the forest, ordained by Time. He remained with Sita and Lakshmana near the sea. Once the God Fire appeared to Him in the form of a Brahmana.

Story 7: The shadow Sita

Fire, in a Brahmin-form, saw Rama Chandra morose and became himself mortified. Then the pious Fire introduced himself as Agni, and addressed the truthful Ramachandra, "O Bhagavan Ramachandra! I now speak to you how time is now coming to you. Now your Sita will be stolen. The course of Destiny is irresistible; none else is more powerful than Time, or Fate. So, give over your Sita, the World Mother to me and keep with you this Chhaya Sita (the shadow Sita; the false Sita). When the time of Sita's ordeal by fire will take place, I will give Her back to you." Ramachandra heard Fire and gave his assent. But his heart shattered. By the yogic power Agni (Fire) created a Maya Sita. She was perfectly equal to the real Sita. Fire, then, handed this Maya Sita to Ramachandra. As per some sources, Vedavathi was born as the shadow Sita.

Agni (fire) took the real Sita and said, "Never divulge this to any other body" and went away. What to speak of divulging the secret to any other body, Lakshmana even could not know it.

Soon after, Rama saw one deer, made of all gold. To bring that deer carefully to her, Sita sent Ramachandra with great eagerness. Putting Sita under Lakshmana's care, in that forest, Rama went himself immediately and pierced the deer by one arrow.

That Maya mrigal (the deer created by magic powers) on being pierced, cried out "Ha Lakshmana!" and seeing Hari before him and remembering the name of Hari, quitted his life. The deer body then vanished; and a divine body made its appearance in its stead. This new body mounting on an aerial car made of jewels, ascended to Vaikuntha.

That magic deer was in its previous birth, a servant of the two gate-keepers of Vaikuntha. Because of some reasons, he had to take up this Rakshasa birth. He again became the servant of two door-keepers of Vaikuntha.

On the other hand, Sita Devi, hearing the cry "Ha Lakshmana!"

became very distressed and sent Lakshmana in search of Rama. No sooner did Lakshmana get out of the hermitage; the irresistible Ravana coming as a Brahmana took away Sita forcibly to the city of Lanka (Ceylon).

Now Ramachandra, seeing Lakshmana on the way in the forest, became merged in the ocean of sorrows and without losing any time came hurriedly to the hermitage where he could not find Sita.

Instantly he fell unconscious, on the ground; and, after a long time, when he regained his consciousness, he lamented and wandered here and there in search of Her. After some days on the banks of the river Godavari, getting the information of Sita, he built a bridge across the ocean with the help of His monkey armies.

Then he entered with his army into Lanka and slew Ravana with arrows with all his friends. When Sita's ordeal by fire came, Agni (Fire) handed over the real Sita to Ramachandra. The Shadow Sita then humbly addressed Agni and Rama Chandra, "O Lord! What am I to do now? Settle my case."

Story 8: Story of birth as Draupadi

She was advised to go to Pushkar, and do penance there. Hearing this, the Chhaya Sita went and practised Tapasya for the three divine (lakh) years and merged in Maha Laksmi.

Vedavathi, the incarnation in part of Laksmi dissolved in the body of Kamala. This Svarga Laksmi appeared at one time from the yagya Kunda (pit). She was known as the daughter of Drupada and became the wife of the five Pandavas.

While this Chaya Sita was practising austerities in Puskara, she became very anxious to get a good husband and asked from Maha Deva the boon 'Grant me a husband' and repeated it five times.

Siva, the chief among the humorous, witty persons, hearing this, said 'O Dear! You will get five husbands.' and thus granted her the boon. Therefore, she became the dearest wife of the five Pandavas.

She was Vedavathi, the daughter of Kushadhvaja in the Satya

Yuga; Sita, the wife of Rama and the daughter of Janaka in Treta Yuga; and Draupadi, the daughter of Drupada, in the Dvapara Yuga. As she existed in the Satya, Treta, and Dvapara Yugas, the Three Yugas, hence She is Trihayani.

CHAPTER 34
CONCLUSION

While there is no system of worship of women in most of the modern religions, we are proud of the fact that Hinduism is rich in the number of Goddesses. We have been worshiping mother power since the time of Vedas and Upanishads.

The basic concept of Brahm or Purusha encompasses both masculine, and feminine forms and also neuter gender for all animate and inanimate creations. It also covers the form of Ardhanarishvar, combining both masculine and feminine powers.

Then, we have concept of Prakriti and Shakti as feminine forms of Brahm, and she manifests in innumerable forms. It is really amazing that Mahamaya is considered the most powerful and controlling deity even above the Tridevas.

Besides the awesome and entertaining stories of the goddesses, we have narrated the stories of great sages, the Rishikas who brought Veda Richas to us, and also of other women scholars.

Presence of all these great ladies in our culture is not myth, or one time inclusion. We find innumerable hymns from Vedas, Brahmanas, Upanishads and other scriptures glorifying women. Is not it then surprising that our current generations have accepted the myth created by so-called historians and social-science experts trained by British education that Women are not having equal rights in Sanatan Dharma, and they are to be controlled every time.

Fie upon these so-called scholars and fie upon we for thinking in this way, and accepting whatever these so-called intellectuals have propagated as our culture.

I am sure that readers of my earlier parts of this series are no more ashamed of the negative aspects propagated by these forces about Hinduism about multiple Gods, and Idol worship.

This part of the series proves that never in the glorious history of Sanatana Dharma, women were disrespected, or considered unequal to men. And, we have now ample examples to prove that the women in India always had the right to read every scripture, and to perform every Yagya.

ABOUT THE AUTHOR

Kaushal Kishore

Kaushal Kishore, M. Sc., CAIIB is a Retired Executive from NABARD, the apex agricultural and rural development finance institution of India. He is a CFA (Chartered Financial analyst), and a FRM (Financial Risk Manager) certified by GARP (Global Association of Risk Professionals). He has very good experience in Rural banking, Microcredit, Project financing, Supervision, Institutional Development, and Risk Management.

The author is passionate since his childhood about spiritual and religious learnings from ancient Scriptures including Vedas, Upanishads, and Puranas. After his retirement, he has devoted himself to the deep study of these scriptures.

Analysis of the wisdom available in these books has made him confident that there is a huge need of identifying and presenting the pearls of wisdom from Indian scriptures. It will be highly beneficial for humanity, particularly for Indians in modern times.

He is of the view that we need to make available these gems of wisdom in Hindi, English, and modern Indian languages. He has volunteered himself to such a noble cause.

One may contact author through his email kkishore.frm@gmail.com.

His website contains very popular blogs on Vedanta Philosophy, and other religious subjects https://www.kaushal-kishore.com

Other books published by the Author
Kaushal Kishore has already authored five books in English and

published all these books in Hindi as well. A brief of his books is presented below

"Madhu Vidya: Straight from Horse's Mouth" is published as an e-book in both Hindi (ASIN: B0CHFK1CMZ) and English (ASIN: B0CG6VR5WM), and as Paperback and as Audiobook.

The book is narrating some wonderful stories from Puranas and Brahmana Granth and a superb wisdom famous as "Madhu Vidya" known as essence of all wisdom.

The book, which emerged as best seller, has global links mybook.to/MADHU and mybook.to/MADHU-HINDI

A three-book series on "Eternal Meditation Principles: Brahm Vidyas" both in English and as "Dhyaan Ke Shaashvat Siddhant: Brahm Vidyas" in Hindi.

The series narrates the best pearls of wisdom from major Upanishads in a very simple and relatable way, along with the system of Meditation as in Patanjali Yog sutra, and Bhagavad Gita, and explains the concepts of Advaita Vedanta Philosophy and the way to realize Moksha, based on Shankaracharya's teachings.

The first part of the series is published as an eBook in English (ASIN: B0CM1CT5J8), and Hindi (ASIN: B0CR141X9F-Hindi), and as paperbacks and audiobooks.

The second and third part have also been published both as eBooks in English (ASIN: B0CVNG8WNW, ASIN: B0CYTMZGTF) and Hindi (ASIN: B0CXK89ZCZ, ASIN: B0D5ZN46S9), and as Paperback.

Global links are mybook.to/EMP-1, mybook.to/EMP-2, and mybook.to/EMP-3 for English and mybook.to/EMP-HINDI-1, mybook.to/EMP-HINDI-2, and mybook.to/EMP-HINDI-3 for Hindi books.

These books have emerged as Best-sellers in their Groups.

Both parts of the current series, named "Stories from Puranas: Part 1" and "Stories from Puranas: Part 2" are also best sellers in Amazon. Links are mybook.to/Purana1, and mybook.to/Purana2 respectively. Hindi edition link is mybook.to/Purana-HINDI-1, and mybook.to/Purana-Hindi-2. All are published as

paperback also.
The Amazon Author page of Kaushal Kishore is
https://www.amazon.com/author/kaushal.kishore

Made in United States
Orlando, FL
16 April 2025

60575614R00122